My Egypt

MY EGYPT
WHY I LEFT THE EX-GAY MOVEMENT

Ben Tousey

authorHOUSE™

1663 LIBERTY DRIVE, SUITE 200
BLOOMINGTON, INDIANA 47403
(800) 839-8640
WWW.AUTHORHOUSE.COM

Also by Ben Tousey

THE WARRIOR
  A science fiction fantasy about the end of the world
STOLEN WINE
ACTING YOUR DREAMS
  An Actor's Guide to Dream Interpretation

First published by AuthorHouse 01/11/06

ISBN: 1-4259-0549-8 (sc)

Printed in the United States of America
Bloomington, Indiana

This book is printed on acid-free paper.

Library of Congress Cataloging-in-Publication Data

Tousey, Ben D
My Egypt: Why I Left the Ex-Gay Movement

1.) Ex-Gay: 2.) Exodus International: 3.) Gay: 4.) Reparative Therapy: 4.) 9/11:

Contents

In the Beginning

It was late September, 1984. Only a few more days until I turned 19 years old, and in Riverton, Wyoming—in 1984, old enough to legally drink. I had spent most of my teenage life counting the days until I could walk into a bar and show my ID without being thrown out, or purchase alcohol myself and not have to spend hours trying to find someone to buy it for me. My day of freedom was almost upon me and I awaited it with zealous anticipation.

That's what was on my mind this late evening as my younger sister Rachel, her boyfriend Pete, and I made our way from Riverton, to Lander, a mere twenty-four miles away. Now Wyoming is nothing like most states as far as population goes. Riverton had a population of about 15,000 and Lander had a population of 8,000 (when Mrs. Robert's family was in town for the family reunion). Unlike today's modern cities which go from town to town without leaving civilization, a trip between towns in Wyoming was a lonely one, and so there were very few people on the roads this night, and no other lights.

Listening to AC/DC, Back in Black through the stereo, my favorite album at the time, deep inside me something else was going on. Even though I was only 18, I was tired—worn out, afraid, lonely, and worst of all, lost and confused. I was lost in the confusion, lost in the loneliness, and lost in helplessness. As Pete drove his Gremlin (boy did that have a cool stereo system), I sat silently listening to the dulcet tones of "Hell's Bells" at a nearly deafening level looking up through the clear autumn night at the stars, which were so bright, and so thick, but so far away. While looking at the sky that autumn night, a thought crossed my mind, and I very quietly voiced it. "God," I said, "I don't know if I can change who I am, and I don't know if I want to. But if you want me just like this, then I guess that's okay."

I looked up at the stars, kind of expecting them to fall toward the car, or spell something grand in the sky, but nothing happened. A few stars winked, but it wasn't for me. But deep inside, as I sat there, with heavy metal blaring at ear-splitting volumes, something inside of me went still. It was quiescence in a place that I hadn't felt for some time. I felt that maybe God did want me, even if I didn't plan on changing. Pete noticed that I had gotten quiet, so I quickly rectified the situation by joining in with a rousing chorus of "You Shook Me All Night Long."

I never told anyone about that night, and we finished our trip to Lander just as we had started. That sense of peace was gone, but in its place was a small kernel of hope slowly taking root in emotional soil I had never been aware of before.

Coming Home Again

Why wouldn't God want me? I wasn't a murderer! I wasn't a thief! (Well, there was that one time. It was a candy bar, and I paid for it. It cost eighty dollars by the time the judge got done with me.) I didn't pick on animals or children, and I wasn't a Satanist. (Mike Warnke was a Satanist, and God accepted him.) I did have some problems, though. I drank a lot, I had issues with drugs, I'd been kicked out of school on several occasions, my parents and I fought most of the time; and I was known by my friends as a partier, and by the "establishment" as "bad seed." I lied about where I was going to my parents, and I sometimes stole money to buy alcohol. But those were minimal. That was nothing compared to what I heard when I listened to Mike Warnke albums. What could be worse than being a Satanist? I'd heard hundreds of stories (including Mike's) growing up about people much worse than me finding God, and huge crowds of people would flock to see them as they recounted their traumatic stories of deliverance. In reality there wasn't anything in my mind that could keep me from God—except for one thing.

Let's start at the beginning—no, let's not. That would take too long, and why wait? There was something going on in my life that I couldn't talk about to anyone, not even to God. At eighteen, I desperately wanted to have sex. What eighteen-year-old didn't? But this was different. I wanted to have sex with a man. I wanted to have sex with someone of my own gender. Every good-looking guy I saw at that time in my life sent my head into creative fantasy about togetherness and closeness—and—sex.

In high school, while all my friends were dating, I wasn't. I had a girlfriend or two, but the bottom line was that I couldn't get into it. While my guy friends talked about their sexual exploits with their girlfriends, I had to make mine up, and hide the fact that I would really rather be having my sexual exploits with them.

Growing up in Riverton, Wyoming, it wasn't a good idea to talk about that kind of thing. Riverton was almost directly in the center of the state, and it wasn't really influenced by the country around it. The population consisted of mostly farmers and ranchers, Native Americans… and straight people.

Most of you know my story. You've heard it many times. You've heard it so many times in fact that when you think you're about to hear it yet again, your eyes glaze over and you start daydreaming about Amy Grant with a halo in a white, tight-fitting choir robe.

At that point in my life I was coming from a fairly religious background. My mom and my step dad were both Seventh-Day-Adventists, and naturally, that would mean I was one too. I was even baptized into the Adventist Church when I was in Junior High.

I knew that God had heard my prayer that night in the Gremlin with Pete and Rachel because of a small miracle that happened a few days later. All my life I had wanted to write songs. I loved playing the piano, but even more than that, I loved writing music, even though most of what I had written was hardly noteworthy (no pun intended). In fact, my songs were downright bad. But on this night, I was sitting at the piano playing random cords and notes, and before I knew it a melody had begun to blossom in my head and through my fingers out to the piano. As the melody flowed, so did the song lyrics. I quickly ran and got some paper and a pen and began writing as fast as I could to keep up.

Within an hour, I had a song. This particular song was what I would call my first real song; the first song I ever wrote with any kind of substance. It was far advanced from many of the other songs I would write later after I had developed greater songwriting abilities. This song was called "Coming Home Again," and it reflected my feelings of abandoning my childhood beliefs in God and striking out to find life on my own. As I played it my eyes welled up with tears. I was home again. God did want me, he gave me a song, and I was about to embark on a journey that would take me deep into the heart of God.

But on this adventure I had to find a way to deal with the one thing I wasn't sure I could change, just as I had spoken of in my prayer that night, with the stars as my witnesses. There was no denying that I wanted to sleep with men. But now that I was truly accepted as God's own, I must change that. I must reorient my sexual orientation. And from that day on I would invest all my efforts in counseling or some form of reparative therapy (reparative therapy is the term used in counseling homosexuals in an attempt to change their orientation).

It Was Your Father's Fault

Right away, whenever I talk to anyone about my sexual struggle, the phrase "It was your father's fault" is the first thing I hear. Some are convinced that the reason I'm gay is because I had a bad relationship with my father. And they're partly right; my relationship with my father wasn't all that great. In fact, what I can remember of it was downright miserable.

As with any life story, I started my life young and innocent, but I soon grew out of that. I was born in a hospital in Whitefish, Montana, and it all went to hell from there. There were three of us kids, me, the oldest, Rachel the girl, and the middle child, and Brian, the youngest. We were born pretty close together, with only fourteen moths separating me and my sister, and barely three years separating me and my younger brother. Brian, the youngest, was born with a very bad heart defect.

When I was about six, my mom and dad divorced. To this day I remember almost nothing about my father, but I am told by all those who knew him that he was a very abusive man, and according to them, I was the focus of much of his wrath. I remember enough though, and that's why there hasn't been much of a relationship between us.

Whenever I get together with my extended family, I hear from them in that self-righteous tone telling me how important it is to forgive him and learn to love the man that they all know and love. I'd like to see them live with him as his child and then see how easy their rhetoric would be. And I will address the area of forgiveness later on, and my work in that area.

There was no denying that this man wanted nothing to do with me. I remember many times after the divorce wanting to go and see my father, but I couldn't because he didn't want to see us. (My mom did try and make up stories that he was busy, but even then, I knew better.) I remember that hurt me as a child, and I cannot describe the emptiness I felt because of that. (Eventually I gave up on him and by the time I was in junior high, I had no second thoughts about ever seeing him again.)

I have snatches in my memory of him when he lost his temper. I have one particular memory of him beating my mother and the two of them screaming, and all I could do was hide in my room.

Growing up, my mom was poor, and she worked hard to make sure her kids were taken care of. She didn't waste her money, she wasn't out boozing at the expense of us kids, but she didn't have a lot to feed us with outside of food stamps. At this time my dad was supposed to be paying child support, which he refused to do. So in frustration, the state of Montana arrested him for back child support. His family was living on food stamps, and it wasn't uncommon for us to have to stretch our meals so they would last. My father informed my mom that he would rather sit in jail than pay a dime in child support. So the state released him, realizing that they weren't going to get anything out of him.

When I reached the age of 9, my mother met and married Roger, a friend of our cousins. Roger was a Seventh-Day-Adventist, and I suddenly found myself banned from Saturday morning cartoons, pepperoni pizzas and Coke-a-Cola. (Seventh-Day-Adventists have church on Saturdays, and they aren't allowed to eat pork... nor are they allowed to drink caffeine.) I went from belonging to a family that consisted of mom and three kids, to mom, step dad, three kids, and two stepsisters.

Naturally Roger and I didn't get along too well. Roger was a carpenter, who worked with his hands and loved to get dirty. I didn't like working with tools. I wanted to be an actor, or a musician. Dirt was never a problem for me. I could get as dirty as the next boy. In fact, I loved the dirt. I would build roads and drive play trucks. My friend Toby and I would turn on the water at his farm and let it run down a little "riverbed" we dug in the dirt. Then we'd build a huge dam and build a city under the dam while the reservoir was filling up. Once we got a fair amount of water, for fun we would break the dam and watch as a wall of water descended upon our hapless residents and destroyed our play city. It didn't matter where I was; if there was water, and if there was dirt, then I was playing in it.

Roger moved us into a one-bedroom shack behind his "shop," half way between Columbia Falls, and Whitefish, Montana, and that was our home for a very long time. When we first moved in, there was no running water, no heat outside of a wood stove in the basement, and all seven of us slept in one room. Every day we went down the hall to the kitchen to eat, and then went back to the room to sit. Those were the only two rooms in the house aside from the bathroom. Eventually, Roger hung up a curtain so we could have some "privacy" while we did our business. But on the up-side, we weren't being polluted by all that trash on TV, since we didn't have one.

Not knowing any better, I thought that all of this was normal. Every Saturday morning we were carted off to church, and I sat in Sabbath School and listened as the teacher told us how God had called the Seventh-Day-Adventists to be his chosen church in the last days, and Ellen G. White to be his "Last Days Prophet," and that I should never turn my back on the church or I would burn in the Lake of Fire at the last days. (Adventists didn't believe in an everlasting hell, they believed in one great conflagration at the end of the thousand year millennium after the persecution of the Adventists.) They talked about other stuff too, but when you're 10 and you have these visuals of standing outside the New Jerusalem burning while your loved ones look on simply because you picked a different church to attend, it's pretty hard to focus on anything else.

My little brother, as I mentioned earlier was three years younger than me and had been born with a serious heart defect. We all knew about this, but somehow Brian managed to function quite normally for most of his life. But as he reached six and seven, the heart defect started taking its toll on his body and he was sent to the University of Washington hospital in Seattle, for surgery. Brian died the next night after the surgery, and when I was ten years old, I learned that my little brother would never come home again. I never forgot that day, or that phone call. I was staying with my aunt Mary in Montana, and my mom called from Seattle to tell me that "Brian was sleeping with Jesus." (Adventists also believe that the dead stay dead until Jesus returns, and then they all rise together with the living to meet Jesus in the Air at the second coming.) But no matter how I thought of it, it still hurt. Sleeping with Jesus or not, he was never waking up.

After Brian's death I learned what kind of man my father really was. He paid for Brian's funeral, and then deducted the funeral costs from the child support he owed my mother (which he had never paid). But Roger wasn't much help either. He couldn't wait to spend all the money that came pouring in from friends and family members to convey their sympathies and help offset funeral costs.

So I suppose you could say that it's true, the men in my life weren't the greatest. But there is one man who did step in and try to offset the trauma. That man was my grandfather. At the time it was happening I didn't realize it, but as I look back, I can see how my grandfather tried so hard to be a good surrogate father. He would come often and pick us kids up and take us to his house. He took me and Brian fishing. (This was especially hard on him because I couldn't sit still in the boat, and that would drive him crazy.) He let us work with him out in the yard. He took us down to the lake to play. He took us out for pizza. Unfortunately, there was some strain in our relationship during my high school years, and he never did know why, and I kind of wish that he did, so he could understand that I wasn't ungrateful for all that he did.

When I was 10, Roger took a job with the Adventist Church as a Bible Salesman selling Ellen G. White Books in Lander, Wyoming. So the family was moved from Kalispell, Montana, where the rest of our family lived to our new residence in Wyoming. We moved into a house smack on a farm owned by our landlords. Our family of four children (now down by one), and my mom and Roger. Our family added bulk to the little Adventist church school built directly behind the church.

It was Your Mother's Fault

Well if it wasn't your father's fault, then it has to be your mother's fault. After all, it doesn't just happen; somebody had to start this mess.

After the divorce, my mom went a little crazy, partying, having fun, meeting men, and leaving us with aunts and uncles and grandparents. I still remember the day we were carted to the hospital to see her because she had fallen asleep at the wheel and rolled off an embankment while on her way to work. It was a serious accident, but she survived.

It was in this period of her life that my mother became "born again." We kids, I, my younger sister Rachel, and my youngest brother, Brian, spent some very interesting times in some very interesting churches after that. She was saved during the "Jesus Movement" of the early seventies, and that meant that the churches she attended were actively engaged in speaking in tongues (which involved a lot of spitting), laying on of hands (which involved a lot of slapping), and other charismatic activities such as jumping and dancing and lifting of hands in the air (which involved a lot of swinging back and forth). While this was frightening to me at first, I soon got used to it.

Then she met Roger. As I mentioned earlier, Roger was a Seventh-Day-Adventist. My mom rejected the church at first, but Roger eventually wore her down, and before long, she was an active participant in the church.

In the fourth grade, I was pulled out of public school, and placed in a Seventh-Day-Adventist Church School to prevent me from being tarnished from the world. I think there were two catalysts for this event. The first one happened when I came home from the library one day with a book on magic, and that freaked my mom out. (I'll talk a lot more about this later, but for now, magic is tantamount to calling on the Devil and offering him your soul in certain circles, and is punishable by death in the Old Testament, and everlasting hell fire in the New Testament.)

The second catalyst was a conversation I had with my brother in front of my mom. In the process of this conversation, I was so eloquently explaining the history of the Grand Canyon. I started out telling my little brother that the Colorado River used to run along the top of the desert on flat ground. Then, slowly over hundreds and millions of years, it started to cut a hole into the ground and formed the Grand Canyon. That was the last straw for my poor mother. Next thing I know I'm church-school where my mind would not be corrupted by the lies of evolution. "I can't believe they would take God out of his own creation" was her mantra.

My First Experience with a Homosexual?

Before my mom met Roger, but after she became a born again, she met two ladies in a church we were attending who were trying to start a music ministry. Their names were Bernadette and Brenda. We loved Bernadette and Brenda. They were the sweetest ladies. They were a couple of big ladies who would sing together and play their guitars (folk music of course). Bernadette and Brenda were always together. I don't remember ever seeing them apart. They had a motor home that they lived in and that they traveled in to their gigs at various churches in the state of Montana (are you seeing a pattern here?).

I can't really say that they were lovers, but as I looked back on my life after the many changes of coming out, I can't help but wonder. "Were they, or weren't they?" The reality is I don't really know, but I was curios. "Why?" you might ask. "Because," I might answer.

As soon as we moved to Lander, Wyoming, we were put into the local Seventh-Day-Adventist church-school almost immediately. I'll never forget Mrs. Gordon, the teacher at the school. She was probably in her early thirties at the time. Our school was very small, and consisted of only a handful of families. The two biggest families were ours, which consisted of four kids (by that time my brother had passed away) and the Garretts (which had six kids, although only two of them were in school with me). Then there were the smaller families.

In this particular school, though it was small, there was a lot of politics, and I must say, the parents of the students were as childish (if not more so) as the students themselves. And while I never heard her say anything, looking back it had to have made Mrs. Gordon's life a living hell. She only lasted two years before she got out of there, and I can't say that I blame her. But she was amazing to me. Maybe that was because she saw something in me that I wasn't aware of yet, but it was definitely beginning to show itself.

By now I was in Junior High, and certain behavioral changes were starting to take place (I was a little limp-wristed, and not very boy-like), and these changes were noticeable to the people around me. For the most part I don't remember thinking too much about them because they seemed natural to me. I didn't realize that I was acting and behaving so differently, but everyone else saw it, and they acted very strangely toward me. I just thought they didn't like me because I was weird (which, in all reality I would have to say was mostly true).

Mrs. Gordon saw something in me, and while I've never been able to confirm that, I truly believe it. It was the way she treated me. Rather than go after me for my odd behavior (as so many teachers before her had), she seemed to encourage me in her own little ways. I remember one day I had a meltdown and got in trouble with the teacher's aide. When Mrs. Gordon returned, she wasn't happy with me. But something happened at the moment and despite every effort to control myself, I broke down and started to cry. She was there immediately with her arms around me trying to comfort me.

Mrs. Gordon had a roommate in Iowa where she lived before she moved to Wyoming (I think it was Iowa). She told us that this roommate was going to be joining her in Lander soon. When Marsha arrived, she was butch. Nobody in the small town of Lander thought anything of it though. It wasn't until many years later after I had come out that I even had the epiphany, but looking back, Marsha was the stereotypical lesbian. She lived in blue jeans, kept her hair very short, talked like a guy, and knew more about cars than anyone else in Lander (including my step dad, Roger, who thought he was the penultimate mechanic). There wasn't a bicycle in our school that she wasn't willing to fix. And many is the time she would bend over to take a look at a bicycle chain or a wheel, and, what do you know, there was a half moon, shining proudly for all of us kids to see.

While Mrs. Gordon was able to reach out to me, the rest of the church wasn't. I didn't quite fit the Adventist motif. I was, according to them, a rebel. I don't even remember what it was that set me apart, except that my relationship with Roger was steadily going downhill as I got older. And I listened to "that Rock and Roll." Back in those days Rock and Roll was an incarnation of Satan (I think they still believe that) and Disco caused homosexuality in laboratory rats.

Our family dysfunction continued to get worse, and needless to say, Roger knew how to play on the sympathy of the church. I was sent home from school many times during my junior high school years. When I was in the seventh grade Mrs. Gordon left the Lander school (can you blame her?) and in came Mr. Davies. This guy was bizarre. There's just no other way to describe him. The gap between me and Roger was deepening and the violence was getting worse.

It was shortly after that, that we learned that my step sisters' mom was living with a lesbian lover. Of course we never told anyone about it for fear of the scandal it would make at church, but it was a topic of constant conversation in our house from time to time. So needless to say, it looked as if homosexuality was all around me, though I didn't know it, even in Wyoming.

My History with God

As a very young child, I somehow related to God. My aunt tells me that she was always telling me I had to go home because I was telling the other kids about Jesus, and it pissed her off (this was before my mom got "born again"). I don't remember that, but I do remember being enamored by Jesus. He was my friend. I had this sense of him that I could never quite explain as a kid, and again, I didn't think anything of it.

After my mom became born again, I followed her lead as if it were natural. I remember one time my grandmother called me a Jesus freak. I told her that a Jesus freak was "someone who loves the Lord more than you." That didn't make my grandmother too happy, but my mom got a laugh.

Then along came Roger and the Adventist church. Suddenly it wasn't enough just to love God. Now I had to walk this fine line of behaviors and attitudes. And most importantly, I couldn't go to any other church, not even with friends to special events. I was puzzled about that because now I had to come to terms with the idea that all these other friends of my moms were actually being deceived by the Devil, and would turn us in to the government when the

Anti-Christ took over. No longer was God a friend, but now he was an austere father whom you had better not piss off (that's my word, nobody in our church would have dared to speak like that). And I couldn't eat pork, and I couldn't watch TV on Saturdays, I couldn't drink Coke or go to movies. That may be where I started to develop that "love-hate" relationship with God, I'm not really sure. But I did still love him. My little mind reached out to him in a way that was uncharacteristic for what was happening in my life.

After my little brother died, my relationship with God met its first major roadblock. We had spent hours, days, weeks, years, praying that God would heal Brian, and we really had faith that this would happen. But Brian didn't come out of that surgery. This taxed my relationship with God. Before that, I could trust God. Sure he didn't give me the horse I had asked for, but when I needed to leave my bike unattended, I knew that I could "plead the blood of Jesus around it," and it would be safe (and it always was). But now when I really needed something from God, it wasn't there. I could no longer trust him.

I was also struck with some serious guilt over the whole experience. To be honest, I was jealous of Brian and the attention he got from the rest of the family. Sometimes when we would get in fights, I could say some ugly things, and now that he was gone, I had to live with some of those ugly words and because he was dead, I could never apologize for them. I don't think I ever admitted it publicly, but it really took a toll on me spiritually and psychologically.

After we moved to Wyoming, I continued to serve God without questioning him too much. In the Adventist church, Ellen G. White was considered God's last great prophet, and so I read her books. I took her word as gospel, and I would fantasize about being a prophet myself. Something very deep inside of me wanted to be recognized as a spiritually wise person. (That was before I read that all the prophets were killed in gruesome ways and that their lives were mostly miserable—but that's another story.) I don't know if this was because I wanted people to respect me, or if it was because I really wanted to hear God the way Ellen G. White claimed to. I wanted to go into vision and see angels and hear God's voice speak to me, and know what was beyond this life. In short, I was looking for some "connection" to God. I daresay, I may have even been looking for the "father" that I hadn't experienced in my own life.

During this period of time, I really wanted to be a good kid and make God happy. I liked hearing the Bible stories, and in my mind they came to life. I couldn't understand how Eve could have possibly trusted a snake. "What was she thinking?" I was enamored with the story of David and Jonathan. There was something about their relationship that made me relate to them. Being naïve still, I didn't realize what was going on emotionally, but it really began to pull at some interesting emotional needs. I used to fantasize about having a friend like David, or like Jonathan, someone who was so close that we could physically hold each other. But it hadn't led to anything sexual, and I wasn't yet aware that this was bad, or where it was leading.

Despite all this, or because of all this, I was considered rebellious by Roger and his church friends. Maybe it was the Rock and Roll or the Disco.

IT'S NOT A CHOICE... IT'S A DISCOVERY

It's the hymn of the Christian whenever the topic of homosexuality arises, and it's usually said by people who have never come into contact with homosexuals (or never really listened to them). "Homosexuality is a choice" they intone in their best James Dobson voice. But up to now, I hadn't made any choices along those lines.

While people believe that, every gay and lesbian person I know would have done anything to have found a way to change. What person in their right mind would choose to go through what most gay men and women go through in their lives? My friends also have a song: "Who would choose this?" they ask. The truth is we didn't get a choice. If you listen to the stories of those growing up gay, you will find that they have tried very hard to change their orientation. Most of the guys I know tried sleeping with girls. Many of them even got married, thinking that would solve their problem. Most of the women I know tried sleeping with men. I remember talking to one lesbian friend of mine (I'm sorry, X-Lesbian, she's still out there fighting) and we were joking that if we could only change places. I could be the lesbian, then I could like women and she could be gay and like men.

The first time I remember having any inclination that I might be "different" from all my friends was after the release of the movie "Grease." I was in Junior High School at the time... (Mrs. Gordon was my teacher) and I had to sneak away to see this movie because we weren't allowed to go to the movies because it was forbidden by our church—"When you walk into a movie theater, you're guardian angel is left standing at the door." I was okay with that because I didn't really need him (my guarding angel) while I was watching the movie. It would be later when my parents found out that I went to the movie I would really need him, and I figured by then he'd be there, so it was all good.

During the movie, I could not stop looking at John Travolta. In my mind he was so good looking. At first I thought it was just envy. I thought I just wanted to be like him. But I was also observing how he looked in his jeans and leather jacket. After the movie, when all the boys were talking about Olivia Newton John in her tight leather and going on about how in love they were with her in her new outfit, I suddenly realized that something was very wrong. I wasn't affected by her at all. Okay, she was a very nice looking lady and she could really sing, but her looks did nothing for me. So I joked with my friends about how much I "ached" after seeing her. Then I tried to ignore whatever feelings the movie had stirred up.

But then I had my first "wet dream." Guess who played the starring role in the erotic Dreamplay? You guessed it—John Travolta.

As time went on, it became more and more obvious to me that things weren't going to change. I started becoming keenly aware of the men around me. I found myself looking when I thought they weren't, and thinking about them. Still, I pretended that nothing was wrong.

When it came time for High School, the first semester of my freshman year I was shipped off to Campion Academy in Loveland, Colorado. Campion was a four-year high school for Adventists so that we could attend school without being indoctrinated by any false teaching outside the church.

My first few weeks at Campion were fairly uneventful, but something happened that changed all of that. When I first arrived at Campion, I didn't know anyone, I was far away from home, and I was extremely shy (okay, not extremely, but I hated not knowing anyone). I was also going through that awkward time in my life where hormones were churning, the body was changing, and I was forced to deal with the ups and downs of being a teenager without anyone to tell me what was happening. I felt profoundly out of place. I had no idea that much of this was natural. I thought I was experiencing something that was wrong, and it was only happening to me.

I lived in a dormitory where I was surrounded by other guys. I had a guy as a roommate, I showered with guys, I went to the bathroom with guys, I had my devotions with guys. There were guys all around me, and the school had set it up so that guys and girls didn't have too many opportunities to get together. It was just me and the guys. It was also in this setting that I began to become aware of sexual feelings. Up until then I had been relatively naïve about the subject, even with my unexplainable feelings toward John Travolta. But here at Campion, things were getting more complicated. I was now a teenager, and I was becoming very sexually agitated. But I was very careful never to let my guard down for fear of the consequences.

Somehow, no matter how hard we try, we always emit some sort of fairy dust or some fairy sensory perception (fsp), because the people around us just seemed to know, regardless of our best efforts to hide it. I was standing outside the boy's dorm one day between the dorm and the cafeteria, and Tony and some of his friends were there. I stood there for a few moments waiting for my friend to join me for supper. There was just me, Tony, and his friends. I looked over at Tony. When I did, he shot back with an icy stare and with all the venom he could muster he spit out the word, "Faggot!" That was the defining moment... that was it. I now knew what I was. I was a faggot.

I stood there on the sidewalk looking over at Tony completely stunned, but I didn't know what to say. After a few moments he asked "Aren't you going to say anything?" What could I say? How do you respond to a comment like that? So I turned to face him, took up an old British aristocratic stance, and bowed my best bow toward him. "Thank you" I said, and decided to go in and eat and not wait for my friend. The irony of this whole story was that I had a major crush on Tony's brother. I didn't know it was a crush, I just thought I wanted to be close to him, but after that moment I knew it for what it was.

So that's what was wrong with me. I was fairly sheltered in Lander—now Riverton, Wyoming, but I knew what a faggot was—and it was me. After that day, I started falling apart at school. I started acting up, skipping class, goofing off, and I just stopped worrying about what my teachers thought of me. My attitude went from being one of the better attitudes in the school, to being one of the worst. And after that first semester I was asked to leave the school indefinitely until I could get my act together. On the way home, I was kicked off the bus for bringing a Coke on board. (Seventh-Day-Adventists are adamantly opposed to caffeinated products.) They sure did set the bar low for rebellion.

The next few years were quite turbulent. I was still stinging from Tony's comment, and I was in fear of being physically hurt because of my differences. By this time my family had moved to Riverton, Wyoming and Roger had left his job as a Bible salesman and was working for himself as a contractor. I still hated to work with him, but since I wasn't in school anymore, there was no way he was going to let me lay around and do nothing.

It was also during this time that I discovered alcohol and speed. For the next few years they would be my best friends. I was a speed freak and bordering on alcoholic. There was hardly a day that went by that I wasn't drunk and on something. My favorite type of speed was the Black Beauty, but I also did Cross-tops, Yellow-jackets, Pink-hearts, Christmas-trees—whatever I could get my hands on.

I have struggled with the symptoms of depression all my life (even though I never knew it), and at this point in my life as I look back I could see that those symptoms were very pronounced. I couldn't even get out of bed most mornings. But speed helped me. I could set the alarm fifteen minutes early, turn over, pop a pill, and lie back in bed and wait for the pill to take effect. Then at night I could drink until I couldn't stand up, and pass out somewhere until it was time to go home and start the routine all over again.

Needless to say, things in the family were very difficult. While I may have been struggling with depression (it was diagnosed much later by one of my many therapists, and then confirmed by every therapist thereafter), thanks to the speed and the alcohol, I was now adding some serious mental and physical disturbances to the list. The two biggest were paranoia, and drug induced schizophrenia. On the part of the paranoia, I lived in constant terror that someone was going to find out that I didn't like women (or that I was taking drugs for that matter). While I was on the drugs I could have radical mood changes and sometimes I could get very violent. I never hurt anyone physically, but I could hurt them with words, and I sometimes did.

At that time Roger got the great idea that he could send me to a foster home, where I could live and be out of his way. My mom wasn't going for that. But my mom and I weren't getting along well either. I blamed her for my troubles. It was her fault for marrying Roger whom I really hated at this time in my life. She let Roger move us all the way to Wyoming, and she had to be the reason that I was gay. I never told her any of this stuff, but I felt that way, and I would do anything to get out of the house. I was desperate to be away from both her and Roger.

The first time I ever told anyone about my sexuality, I didn't tell him really. I had met this guy, Mitch, and somehow we became friends. He was just a year or two older than me, and I really looked up to him. He was tall and thin and had curly blonde hair, and he would sit and listen to me talk about just about anything. One night while we were talking, he looked over at me and said—"I know." And then he added, "and it's okay." I knew what he was talking about, but I didn't say anything, not wanting to risk our friendship. A few weeks later Mitch and I were in Jackson Hole, Wyoming visiting Mitch's mother and sister. That night Mitch's sister and another friend went out partying, and Mitch and I stayed home to watch the kids. The kids were asleep and we were in the kitchen. I was sitting on the counter smoking a cigarette and he was standing in front of me. I blew smoke, and he accused me of blowing smoke in his face (in my high school, when you blew smoke in someone's face that meant that you wanted to have sex with them).

"I didn't do it on purpose" I defended myself.

Then Mitch leaned over and kissed me. That was my first kiss ever by a man. My heart was racing my blood was boiling, and I was in another world. It was the most powerful feeling I had ever felt up to then. I couldn't even talk my mouth was so dry and my tongue swelled and wouldn't move. I've never been to heaven, but this was pretty close.

That night when we went to bed, Mitch wrapped his leg around me. My mouth was now arid and I still couldn't talk. I was breathing like a man who had just run a race. I felt as if I was in a dream, but it was the best dream I had ever had.

But things with Mitch were short-lived. Without explanation, he started treating me harshly, ignoring me, and making a point of showing me all the girls he was sleeping with. I had gone from being absolutely ecstatic to almost inconsolable in just a matter of weeks. What made this even more difficult was that I couldn't talk to anyone about it. Nobody knew what Mitch and I had been doing, and I didn't dare tell anyone. So I did my grieving all by myself, with a little help from Jack Daniels and some Coke.

As I began to realize I was gay, I did just that—I began to realize. I didn't decide to fall in love with John Travolta. I was innocently watching him on the screen when all of a sudden I found myself drawn to him the way my friends were drawn to Olivia Newton John. When I had those dreams that boys that age get, instead of involving women, mine involved men. I felt betrayed, even in my dreams.

At the advice of one of my therapists, I tried fantasizing to women in the hope that that would help redirect my orientation. I used Donna Summer, since she was such a powerful icon to me. The problem was, I could focus on her for a brief time, but next thing I know that cop on the Bad Girls album cover would jump into my mind. I found myself thinking about him arresting me and cuffing me, and taking me to his own personal jail—just him and me. All that approach succeeded in doing was to encourage me to get out my Bad Girls album and stare at the cover for hours.

Homosexuality isn't a choice, it's a discovery. The same way heterosexuality is a discovery. A young boy one day discovers that girl's breasts make weird things happen to him in the pit of his stomach. A young girl suddenly finds that she's drawn to a guy because of his looks, or because of his personality. But she begins to realize that it's not just about friendship. She realizes that she wants to be intimate with him. These are discoveries, and most healthy parents don't fault the kids for having these feelings. It's just like growing breasts. Girls don't choose to grow breasts, they just grow breasts. None of us chose to be sexual, we are sexual beings. It's built into us.

The same is true with the gay boy or girl. Suddenly a boy discovers that the look and feel of another boy causes him to feel funny inside, and he starts to tingle in the groin area. The girl sees another girl and wants to be close and intimate. But there's another discovery that goes along with these discoveries. Unlike their counterparts who can express their feelings to their friends, and in some cases their parents, gays and lesbians can't because of their fear of retribution.

Let's look at another aspect about choice. For this I'm going to use as my analogy the example of a computer. Computers work on two basic principles: computer hardware and computer software. Computer hardware is the computer itself. The hard drive, the box it comes in, the chip, the wiring. On a computer, those things cannot be changed. Then there's the software. The software is what runs the computer, like the operating system, a word processor, a graphics program. All these things help the computer do its work, and they can be added or removed as the user feels the need.

So how does this work in real life. Well, let's look at our hard drive. We have our height, our eye color, our hair color, our genetic makeup, our gender. These are things that we cannot change (with a few exceptions). This is our hard drive. What is our software? Our beliefs change from day to day, year to year. We can change where we live, what clothes we wear, who we choose to associate with, what we eat, how much we eat. All these are choices that we can make. This is our software. No matter how much I want to, I will never be able to grow another inch. I can change my hair color, but only through dyes and bleaches, and always the true color will find its way through no matter how I try to change that. That's the nature of things. That's the hardware. Here's an example of how it works. Suppose I told you to stop being straight, and have a homosexual affair? Could you? Most of you couldn't. It would be just too difficult for you. Sexuality is very much located in our hard drives.

FINALLY, SOME SUCCESS

After Campion, God was the last thing on my mind. I came home to Riverton, and tried to fit in with those around me. But I didn't fit in, and before long I had been through three high schools (two of them religious). I was definitely troubled at this point in my life. I was running away from myself even though I didn't know that. And the problem was... wherever I went, I just kept on tagging along.

I ended up in an alternative high school which was geared for kids who didn't do so well in the formal educational system. At least I could pretend that I was in school, and I did, in fact, attend most of my classes most of the time. Granted, I wasn't always sober, but I was there. And I wasn't misbehaving either, so nobody really bothered me. I think deep down inside the teachers there were actually hoping that I would make it, so they took it easy on me.

After a few months in the alternative school, I wanted to attend mainstream high school. As I was sitting with the high school counselor in his office trying to figure out what classes I needed to take, he decided to put me into speech and drama. I needed some English, and he thought these classes would be easy for me. This event would be what Carl Jung would have called synchronicity. Two things happened in speech and drama. I found people that could handle me as I was without any judgment (aside from the typical high school "drama"). They didn't have a problem with my orientation (even though I was still very careful about what I said). For the first time I could talk more openly about what was personal to me. The second point was that I found something I was good at. I started competing in oratory speech and humorous interpretation, and I started winning at speech meets.

This spilled over into other areas of school. For example, I had to keep my grade point average at a certain level, and I had to meet a certain attendance criteria. It was because of that that I started attending classes, and keeping my grades above a C. And my teachers were amazing. I was surprised at how far out of their way they went to make sure that I was eligible to compete.

My science class just happened to start immediately after lunch. This was hard for me to make because I was usually out partying at lunch. I would try really hard to get to class before the bell, but

I was often late. Rather than punish me by knocking my grade down or counting me absent, my science teacher had me write a one-thousand word essay telling him why I wouldn't be late to "a movie," to "catch an airplane," or "to Mr. Tucker's class." So I wrote the article, feeling very much the smart ass. The whole article had a reoccurring theme running through, and read very much like a comedy routine. It turned out he liked it, and told many of my other teachers about it.

I was struggling in my English class because I had missed a couple assignments. My English teacher, Mrs. Heller asked me during class to get a copy of this document I had written for Mr. Tucker. I did, and she read it. I heard her laughing as she did, and at the end of class she had graded it and handed it back to me. This brought my grade up one point so that I could still compete in the next speech meet.

Still I was struggling to get to class on time. Again, after lunch—I had to report to the front office and get a pass so that I could go down the hall to my class. Mrs. Smyth was wondering why she should give me this pass and she asked me why I was late.

"I had a flat tire," I told her.

"That's the fourth flat tire you've had this week," she retorted.

I thought for a minute, and then I looked her dead in the eye and said, "Well, they're all fixed now."

She looked me dead in the eye too. We stood there for a minute looking at each other, and I swear I saw a twinkle in her eye and what looked like a grin start to spread itself across her face.

"Then I guess you won't be having any more flat tires," she finally said and wrote out my pass.

During that time my best friend's step-mom's dad died (I couldn't think of any other way to say it). I remember that we were over at the house and she was talking about it. That's when I told her about my own brother, Brian. As I talked casually about the event, I was drawn back to the time that it happened. I remembered all the guilt and harsh words I had spoken, I remembered the fights and the competition between us for attention. Then I remembered the day we visited his him in the funeral home. I'll never forget seeing his body laying there in the casket. I tried so hard at ten years old to understand why he couldn't open up his eyes and talk to me. His body was there just the way I had remembered it, but he was gone, and I couldn't figure out where he went or why God would take him away (I was especially troubled that God would take away Brian but leave his body). That seemed cruel to me at the time.

The wound opened up and the junk came out. I released the guilt, the anger with God, that sense of abandonment, and I recalled the memory of his little body laying cold in the casket, and how I wished that I could just hold him there and comfort him. For the first time in my life I talked about it. At seventeen, seven years after the event, I had finally opened up to someone.

It was through this process of opening up, and being able to talk about what I was feeling that I started letting go of the drugs. I remember one night I had taken four black beauties, and I thought I had overdosed. As the night went on I suddenly felt some very sharp pains in my chest, and I thought I was going to die. This was very disturbing to me, because I really thought I was going to have to stand in front of God and he was going to condemn me to hell. I wasn't quite ready for that just yet. It amazed me how brave I was when nothing was wrong, but now that I believed I was really looking into the brink of my own grave, God suddenly took on a whole new persona.

I was hanging out at the local teen hang-out, the Riverton Roller Ranch. As you might have guessed, this was a roller skating rink. Roller skating was popular in the eighties. Even in Riverton, Wyoming. As the night went on, I started to feel the overwhelming effect of the drugs, and I could hardly breathe. Every breath felt labored, as if I was struggling to fill my lungs with air. I started to worry. My body went numb. I kept moving, so that I could keep my mind off the terror that was trying to snatch control of my body and mind.

Then something else happened. There were some guys there who, for whatever reason (and I think we know what reason that was), wanted to fight with me. Next thing I know one of my friends took me by the arm and escorted me out of the building quickly and quietly. We got in his car and he drove me away. I was shaking and I couldn't concentrate, and because of my altered state, I wasn't real clear on what was taking place. My friend wondered if he shouldn't take me to the hospital. But to go there would be to admit that I had taken an illegal substance, and that was an even greater risk to me.

So we drove around for a while until the speed wore off; which it eventually did, hours later.

I decided that I wasn't willing to go through something like that again, and from that moment on, my love affair with speed was over. I'd figure out my own damn way to get out of bed, thank you very much. I still liked to drink, and I couldn't imagine a life without pot, but the speed was gone.

This also became very noticeable to my teachers. They could see that I was more coherent and less strung out. I stopped hanging out at the "fence" during lunch (the fence is where we all hung out to smoke and take pleasure in other illegal chemicals). As a result, I began to notice a change in my relationship with them (my teachers). I had always had the vague suspicion that they were somehow trying to help me, but with the fog gone, I could actually see it. I started having fun in school and expressing myself even more.

Even though things were better for me now, I was still the lone gay man in a small town which didn't really understand or appreciate homosexuality. As I look back on my time in Riverton, I realize that Riverton itself wasn't against me, only a certain few had a problem with it. But it was those certain few who made things the most difficult. I had some good friends who knew the truth about me, and they were willing and able to accept me as a friend. Showing up at parties could be dangerous for me though (especially if I was uninvited). I remember one such party. It was a bon fire/school party (unsanctioned by the authorities) and there were a lot of people there. I went with some other friends but we had to leave quickly because some of the people there weren't happy to see us. As I walked away, someone threw a beer bottle at my head. It missed, but it scared me none-the-less.

Despite the emotional healing I experienced over Brian, I was getting angrier with God. Why would he even consider bringing such a plague on me? I didn't ask to be gay, and I had done so many things trying to suppress it, but it would not go away. And at every turn someone had something derisive to say about it.

It was about this time that the AIDS epidemic broke, only then it was announced as "a new cancer in homosexual men." You guessed it; every Christian I met viewed this as God's judgment on homosexuality. Sodom and Gomorrah were finally being judged, and I listened to the Christians in our town sing with glee the story of God's ultimate judgment. They truly felt that it was about time God did something about this scourge.

I felt like I needed to get even with God for what he was doing to me. So I turned to the one person/entity I knew could hurt him. I tried (literally) to sell my soul to Satan. I did all the spells and incantations, I spilled my blood in the middle of the pentagram, and I drew up a legal contract and signed it with my blood. I wanted fame and fortune, and male lovers, and I figured that Satan would bring them to me. I assumed he'd do anything to get a soul away from God. I knew that I faced the peril burning in hell, but I still had enough of the Adventist teaching in me to make it worth the risk.

The Adventist church believed that Jesus would come back, rescue everyone that was Adventist, and take them to Heaven. At his return, the wicked would die and there would be no one left alive on the earth. During that time, Satan and his minions would roam the planet for a thousand years to think about the destruction they caused, with nobody to tempt. At which point Satan would try to repent, but it would be too late. After this thousand year "millennium," The New Jerusalem would descend on the Mount of Olives which would flatten out like a plate, and all the wicked who were dead would be raised up. They would see the beauty of the New Jerusalem, and Satan would capture his last chance to tempt humankind. They would march against the New Jerusalem and try to take it. At that point, fire would come down from heaven and burn the earth and all that weren't inside the gates of the city. But in this case, the fire would consume all that was evil, not just envelop it for eternity. And then it would die out, and God would recreate earth from his throne at the site of Old Jerusalem.

So I figured I would burn for a while, and then it would be over and I would be gone forever. I didn't care about that. After all, I hated God, why would I want to spend eternity with him—Him and his Homo-Hatin' ways.

So this was my opportunity: my window. This was the one way that I could get even with God, and get fame and money and lots of hunks everywhere I turned. But it never took. I never saw Satan, I never felt Satan, and not one demon entered the room. I had heard all the stories growing up in church about demons attacking people who played with Ouija Boards, and yet here I was deliberately calling them, and there was no answer. I kept trying to fine-tune my approach. Maybe I had the wrong number, or I needed more blood (or less blood), or if I said the Lord's Prayer backwards or became a democrat: but there was no Satan. Talk about depressing. Even Satan didn't want me.

I had friends who believed they were witches and warlocks, and they told me that they had become frightened of me because I had so much "power." But the reality was; the only power I had was hate, and anger, just like Darth Vader: and it was that hate and anger that frightened them and everyone around me.

But there was no dark side, there was no Devil. He didn't show up, and I soon gave up out of futility, which just increased my burning hatred of God. Somehow I knew that God was trying to sabotage my satanic aspirations. But it wasn't because he loved me, it was just another opportunity for him to @#$% with my life.

Now I really hated him!

CLEVELAND

I met Eddie when I was attending the Seventh-Day-Adventist church school in Lander. He and his sister attended the school too. We were both in the same grade. Eddie and I became good friends, and we stayed friends until I went off to Campion. Eddie and I had a lot in common. We both had violent and dysfunctional families, and we were both gay. Only we didn't know that last part about each other at the time.

Eddie lived with his father and his step-mother, just opposite of me. His father was also violent and abusive, and his step-mother was a drama queen. One day she took a knife to herself in an attempt to do enough damage to draw attention, but not so much that she did any permanent damage. Eddie was embarrassed and ashamed, and I was the only person he could talk to about it. I don't know why (but again, probably for the attention), but one day his step-mom started a rumor that Eddie and I, and our other friend Tony, were all involved in some sort of sordid love triangle. Boy did the rumors fly. And every time the stories were told they just kept getting more and more racy. I never knew I could have that much fun. I already had rumors regarding me, but now they were worse. And I couldn't help but wonder what it must have been like for Eddie, to know that his own step-mother started them.

As soon as he was able, Eddie contacted his mom in Cleveland, Ohio, and asked to move in with her. She was very happy to have him, and he moved out there just as the two of us were entering high school. I went to Campion, and he went to Cleveland. We kept in touch, and talked over the phone. We sent letters back and forth (this was before the age of e-mail). We sent pictures of ourselves, and through the course of our correspondence, we opened up to each other. He talked to me at length about Cleveland, and how wonderful it was to walk into a bar and see guys hugging and kissing other guys. That appealed to me. I wanted so badly to find this perfect lover, someone I could be with. But like I said, there were mostly straight people in Riverton.

Eddie invited me to come out and visit, and I started giving it some serious thought. Cleveland would be perfect for me. I could go out there, and find a job as a DJ (that's what I did in Riverton), and I could find that man who would make my life complete. Then I would become famous, and my life would be so wonderful. I'd take over for Rick Dees and branch off into rock and roll and acting, and I'd do talk shows, and move to L.A. and be a big star.

As coincidence—or fate would have it, a high school friend of mine, Mark, stopped by to tell me that he was on his way to Chillicothe, Ohio, and if I wanted to ride along with him I could split the gas and that would get me as far as Columbus, Ohio. From there I could take a bus to Cleveland. That was the perfect plan. I would go away to Cleveland, and I would find a rich boyfriend, who really loved me, and who wanted to take care of me, and we would live happily ever after, and I would never come back to Riverton.

There's something about fantasy that never seems to play out in real life the way it does in our heads. Cleveland didn't turn out like I had hopped it would.

I hadn't really dated in Riverton (men or women). I did try to date (women). It was necessary for me to look as straight as I could. I had three girlfriends in high school, and to be honest they were sweet girls, but I couldn't give them what they wanted. My first girlfriend was Candice. She was this cute, spunky little girl, and I really liked her, so we started going out. But no matter how long I was with her, the most we ever did was lie on the couch and cuddle. She was upset because we were together a whole night, and I never once touched her breasts. Needless to say, she broke up with me.

Judy was a cute blonde girl that I went to school with. While I was dating her, her older sister Josephine started experimenting with a lesbian. Josephine told me about it, and asked me what I thought. At the time I was still pretending to be straight so she wasn't sure how I would handle it. Actually it was weird to me. I couldn't imagine anyone having sex with a girl, let alone another girl. In my mind two girls having sex with each other was double the gross, double the yuck.

After Judy I dated Jill. I even took her to the prom. Later that night, at a party, after I had a lot to drink, I decided that I could actually have sex with her. I looked over at her and told her just that. She was ready, and before I could say anything else, she had me by the hand and had taken me to another room. Now, granted, it was sex, and sex can be a lot of fun no matter who you're with, but when it came right to it, I really wasn't into it. She had to tell me what to do the whole time because I didn't know. For example, her breast; I was interested in them, but not the way a straight man would be. I guess I was good for her because whatever she told me to do, I did it.

So needless to say, my dating skills were rather limited. As a result of not dating, and because I hadn't really been away from home, I wasn't prepared to deal with the realities of real life, especially real life all by myself. My first encounter, Mitch, was the only guy I had ever "known" and that turned out to be pretty much a fiasco. So I had no idea what a relationship was like (outside of my parents, and that's not a lot to go on). This lack of knowledge made the fantasies more believable, but didn't prepare me much for the disillusion.

When I arrived in Cleveland, I found that I took to the city. Instead of being afraid, having come from such a small town, I blended in. I was right at home downtown. Eddie and I went to the bars, and I met some guys, but I was young, inexperienced, naïve, and sometimes just plain stupid. One night I went home with a guy named Mark, but it was his friend Kyle I had been ogling all night. I went home with Mark just because I wanted to get laid. But once we got to Kyle's house (Mark was spending the night at Kyle's), it was obvious that

I was into Kyle, and Kyle was into me. Only Kyle had a boyfriend. Mark was angry and stormed out of the house in a huff, calling me an asshole. He wasn't lying. Based on the way I was behaving that night, that's exactly what I was. But again, I was naïve and stupid. The only thing Kyle and I ever did was make out that night, but the next day I went home, and we only talked on the phone from time to time. I wanted to date Kyle, but there was no way he was going to leave his boyfriend for me.

And that was the **best** experience I had. Like I said, until you date, you have no idea what's involved in dating. There's a lot of rejection, vulnerability, and confused emotion, and that's in a healthy relationship. Since I wasn't aware of that at the time, these occurrences, one by one, only made me feel more isolated. Nothing was going the way I had envisioned in my fantasy. I couldn't even find a job as a DJ. There was a grocery store behind Eddie's house, and they were looking for a carryout, but I wanted to be a DJ, and find a man, and get rich and famous. None of which I could do working at a grocery store.

So as a result, when my friend Mark called me from Chillicothe to let me know that he was headed back to Riverton, I decided to go back with him.

My time in Cleveland had left some marks. On the positive, I could be out, whereas I couldn't in Wyoming. But people play games, and gay men and women are no exception. And I was caught off guard when they started playing them with me (an I was completely thrown off guard when I realized that I was playing them too). Because of my upbringing I think, or because I wasn't willing to look at my experiences in Cleveland honestly, I thought that the games and the way people behaved was just a sign from God that homosexuality was wrong just like everybody had been saying. After all, if you can't succeed in a homosexual relationship, then that is a sure sign that God doesn't sanction homosexual relationships. Of course most of the Christians I know have been married at least twice, so by that argument you could say that relationships in general aren't sanctioned by God.

Another downside of the Cleveland experience was that I became very "gay." I was a flamer. I developed the "lisp," the "swish," the "pitch," and boy could I play the Diva. These were characteristics that would not play well in Riverton, so when I got back home, I had to be very careful to say as little as I could, and to avoid moving too much, and sit with my legs uncrossed and my feet on the floor.

I still had one "official" year of high school left, and when I went to Cleveland it was my intention not to finish (why would a famous DJ need to finish high school?). But I was at least two years behind in credits (from being kicked out of school so many times), and it just seemed like too much work getting caught up. But I decided I might as well finish. There should be one thing in life I finished, and school might as well be it. I ended up taking four or five classes as a home study courses on top of my regular classes so that I could graduate in 1984 (technically only one year later than I should have graduated). I lost my heart for speech and drama, and I didn't feel like competing anymore. I think it had to do with the loss of my naiveté in Cleveland.

Once back in school, in order to get myself to where I could interact with my fellow students without looking like Jack McFarland from Will and Grace (only not nearly as funny), I watched several of the jocks around school, and I used their movements and motions to teach me how to "look straight." This was a little difficult since the jocks didn't like being looked at, especially by a faggot. It was one of the main reasons I skipped gym during my freshman year back in Campion. But I was careful. I learned to rely on my peripheral vision. I could watch them without "watching" them, and it helped. It wasn't long before I was "straight acting." This also took a lot of pressure off of me during my last school year.

THE BEGINNING OF THE END

At home things were starting to unravel. Our family dysfunction had reached epic proportions even for the state of Wyoming. My younger sister had been dating a semi-professional wrestler (the ones on TV who like to throw chairs), and she ran away to Phoenix with him. Roger was becoming more and more violent with me, and I was still drinking way too much and probably on the verge of alcoholism. Roger was now an elder in the Seventh-Day-Adventist Church, and he sure knew how to keep up appearances. At church he was the model of a good Christian, but at home he was violent and abusive.

One day Roger and I had an especially gruesome altercation. Roger's way of dealing with me was through violence. If I pissed him off (which wasn't hard to do), then he liked to throw punches. This particular day he picked me up and threw me across the kitchen. I was so angry that I grabbed a knife and was ready to let him have it. This freaked out everybody else in the house, and suddenly there was a lot of screaming. I knew that I had gone too far, but now I didn't know how to get out of it. So I stood there while he tried to distract me. I wasn't distracted, but I wasn't going to stab him either. So I braced myself.

He grabbed the knife, and next thing I know he was attacking me like a crazed grizzly bear. I managed to get up and out of his grasp, and I took off. I ran out of the house and into town to get away. I didn't want to tell any of my friends, so I just wandered the streets for several hours. My mom eventually found me and drove me home.

Ultimately, the entire family was turned over to the state of Wyoming. Roger was good at educing sympathy, and so it turned out that the state thought that he and his two daughters were victims of me. Roger weighed at least two-hundred-fifty pounds, and he was very strong. At five-foot-eleven, I weighed in at about one-hundred-fifty pounds soaking wet with a heavy down jacket and kneepads. I was so skinny that if I turned sideways and stuck out my tongue I would have looked like a zipper. But somehow I was terrorizing this huge man. Granted I was about three inches taller than him, but my only real physical advantage over him was that I could run faster scared than he could mad.

So I was brought into the social worker's office along with my mom. Edward was the social worker's name, and he looked at me with a rather confused look when I walked through the door. I didn't know what to think of this, but I sat down and listened as he and my mom talked about the family situation. I didn't pay too much attention to their conversation—that is until Edward looked at me and said, "I hear that you're a dope blowing drunk."

That took me by surprise. He was very candid with me. I didn't know quite how to respond. So I looked him straight in the eyes for a moment, and then I told him "I used to be, but I've cleaned myself up."

We held each other's gaze for several seconds, and then he looked back at my mom and they started talking again. It was agreed that my mom and Roger would start counseling. Edward told her that our problems (the kids) were actually their problems (my mom and Roger) and that as soon as they got their lives together, the kids would be just fine.

But Roger only made two counseling sessions, and then he never returned. Meanwhile, my mom was making great strides in her therapy. My sister had been found, and was remanded to the state of Wyoming where she spent a few months in a girl's detention home. Once she was out, her case was again going to go to court where a judge would decide what would happen to her. She wanted to go and live with her father, and the courts would decide if that was possible.

Edward came to the house to visit and check up on the family. Edward and I were getting along quite splendidly by this time. It turned out that we really liked each other. He would often tell me that the reason that Roger and I didn't get along was that emotionally I was much older than Roger. I liked hearing that. Edward and I developed a good relationship over the time he was dealing with our family, and I found him to be a very good and trustworthy friend. He also told me why he had given me such a confused look the first time we met. It turns out, that the way Roger had talked, he had the impression that I must have been about six-foot-ten, four hundred pounds, with arms hanging down to my knees, not this skinny kid who's only chance for survival in a fight would be to run like hell hoping that his attacker wasn't quite as nimble.

As we were touring the house, Edward noticed a large hole in the wall at the top of the stairs. He asked me about it, and I said, "That's where Roger threw me up the stairs." Later he noticed a hole in the wall at the bottom of the stairs. He asked me about that one, and I said, "That's where Roger threw me down the stairs." Then there was the hole in the family room, the hole by my bedroom, some pieces of the kitchen cabinet broken away... all results of a fight between me and Roger.

When the family's situation was brought before the courts of Wyoming, and Edward testified regarding our situation. It was not a big surprise that he didn't have a lot of good things to say regarding the whole mess. Oddly enough though, he had very little to say about me personally. And by the time it was over, my sister had been sent to live in Montana with her father, and the rest of the family was stinging from Edward's assessment. Roger was livid, and it was all he could talk about for weeks. I steered clear of Roger during that time, because I wasn't interested in adding any more holes to the walls of the house.

In the mean time, my mother had decided that if she and Roger were going to work things out, they would have to do it separately. So she separated from Roger. Now when she told me this I should have been excited, but I wasn't. I was terrified. Roger had built us an eighty-five thousand dollar house. This was in Riverton, Wyoming, in 1984. I had my own bedroom for the first time in my life.

That was part of it, but I think that all in all, I was just plain scared. My sister would be leaving Riverton in just a few days to live with her father, and it was going to be me and mother. Just the two of us, and I still had one year of high school left to finish.

All that brought me to that night in September, 1984.

AND THE THERAPY BEGINS

After my mom left Roger, I approached Edward (who also was a therapist), and asked him to counsel me and help me to change my orientation. He was reluctant to do so because he didn't feel it was ethically right, but I insisted. I told Edward that I wanted to love God and serve him with my whole life, and that I didn't' want anything coming between us. Edward told me that it was my explanation that made him feel okay about counseling me (I should point out that Edward was an atheist).

During my remaining years in Riverton, I continued to see Edward. But that wasn't helping. No matter how we talked, or how much time I spent with him, my orientation wasn't changing. Every cute boy I saw would send my heart into palpitations. I nearly ran my car up a light post so many times because I was ogling some guy. Try explaining that accident to the police.

But there was one event in that period of my life that made me seriously consider ending my life because I couldn't deal with my sexuality. It happened one day as I was reading the Bible. I was reading one of the Gospels, and in the story there was the mention of a Roman soldier. In my mind, I suddenly had a visual flash of a Roman soldier in his skirt, with his strong legs and muscular body, and gorgeous face. I was overcome with frustration at that moment.

"God?" I asked. "How can I overcome this thing when even the Bible makes me horny?"

Even the Bible makes me horny! I couldn't believe it. How could I read the very book that was supposed to help set me free if it just made it worse? It was a moment of such utter hopelessness, that I didn't think I was going to be able to face life. Of course today, I realize that it's really a rather funny story, but at the time it was extremely challenging.

But on the upside, my songwriting abilities were really taking off. It seemed that my songs were getting more and more sophisticated. They spoke of God, and how much I wanted to be with him, to be like him, to be near him. I also began to write plays and sketches and short stories (part of this was Edward' idea). He thought that I could really help myself by writing about my feelings and my struggles, and write I did.

I remember one day playing one of my songs for some friends who had gathered around the piano to hear me sing. I sang a song that I had just finished. The title of this song was "In Your Arms (It's Alright)." It was a song that talked about my fears and struggles, but then went into the chorus "When you hold me in your arms it's alright." It was a love song between me and God. When I finished with the song and looked around, there were tears. Just about everyone there was crying.

It was events like this that really helped me to believe that God was with me and he truly was accepting me, and that he was going to bless me as a professional songwriter; eventually (but I had to become straight first). I knew deep down inside that I would never get to be the professional status (which was my greatest dream then) until I dealt with my sexuality (and became straight), and every day I prayed and pleaded and cajoled God to help me find that way out.

Part of my journey back to God involved going back to church. Since the only church I really knew was the Seventh-Day-Adventist church, that's where I returned. But they were not happy to see me. After only a few weeks, I gave up on that church all together.

I made friends here and there, and found a church or two that I didn't mind attending once in a while, but quite frankly I was bothered by what I saw. The churches were varied, but not very healthy. One church that I attended was so austere that it made the Seventh-Day-Adventist church look like a liberal church. Another church I tried out was so into the emotional thing that it really freaked me out. I tried out a church led by a former pimp (and I think he was still working though we didn't know about it at the time). One time I went to church with a friend, and they had a guest pastor. This pastor started going off about how Rock and Roll music was of the Devil. I got pissed off and got up to leave. The pastor actually instructed the other members of the church to try and stop me. At that point I ran as quickly as I could out the door while other members were trying to catch me. At another church I attended it was learned that the pastor there had problems with pornography. He was caught buying pornographic magazines at a local magazine store (but it was straight porn so it wasn't as bad). Another church I attended played some weird mind games. The pastor led his congregation by telling them exactly how to live each and every moment of their lives. He tried that with me, but I was a new Christian just fresh out of the sex and drugs and rock and roll life, and there was still plenty of rebellion in me (in this case, rebellion may have saved me). Needless to say I gave up on finding a church. I was still a Christian, but I found solace in my music, and now my writing. They were my church for quite a while.

During that period of time I met two girls, and both of them had a crush on me. I really liked them too, and so I tried dating them. The first girl I met was Josie. We were both musicians, she played the flute and I played the piano. We would play together from time to time, and we both found it very rewarding. Our friendship blossomed until it became evident that she wanted to go further than that.

The second girl I met was Tina. Tina was a singer, and she loved my music. I was working at a radio station at the time, doing a Christian show called the Gospel Express. This show aired every Sunday morning, and I would play music, and write comedy sketches for it. Tina would listen to my sketches before they aired and give me good advice on how to improve them if they needed improvement. I still remember her laughing so hard at one of my sketches that she nearly spit out her lunch one time while I was previewing it for her.

Eventually I had to tell both Josie, and Tina what I was dealing with because they couldn't understand why I wouldn't have more physical contact with them—or why, when we did have physical contact, it seemed clumsy and insincere. I spent a lot of time with them trying to discover how I could find the healing I needed from God, but still it did not come.

After graduation my mom was transferred with her job to Cody, Wyoming, and I decided that I would move with her. So we moved to Cody, and my sexuality issues came with me. In Cody I met some wonderful people, and I soon found myself in a new church. It was a little wooden building that was the result of an earlier church split. The people there were wonderful people and I took to them right away.

I met one lady in the church who had a healing ministry. In other words, she counseled people, and prayed with them. So I set up some time to talk with her. Edina was a wonderful friend too, and I could trust her. I trusted her with my story, and I trusted her relationship with God to be sincere and real.

While in Cody, and I spent a year with her, trying, if nothing else, just to keep things under control. Occasionally I had bad days, days when I just wanted to go out and find someone who would take me in their arms and hold me close and make love to me. I could talk to Edina about that, and she understood without being judgmental and condemning.

When I talk about this to people now, they're surprised that after all of this counseling, something didn't shift. The best description I can give regarding this struggle is: take a beach ball, fill it with air, and then try to hold it under water. No matter how hard you try, that beach ball is going to do everything it can to get to the surface, and sooner or later you're either going to have to pop it to keep it under the water, or you're going to have to give up and let it surface.

Edina offered me some great advice, and she taught me a lot about expecting from God rather than just hoping that things would work out. So I set out to "expect God to help me go straight." It had an interesting effect on me. It didn't change how I felt about men, but it did make going through the experience a little easier. In the process, Edina prayed for me and cast out a whole plethora of demons that she suspected to be playing a part of the stubborn malady.

Later on that year a guest pastor was in town doing some special revival meetings at our church. His favorite subject was the Devil. Every other sentence was about the Devil. I remember hearing him on several occasions relating how he laughed at the Devil. He laughed at the Devil one time when... then there was the time... and so on and so forth. I was beginning to think that he and the Devil were in the middle of some sort of codependent relationship.

One night after his sermon, he did a questions and answers session where he took questions from the congregation. On this particular night, someone asked about that age old question, the unpardonable sin. They asked him what that sin was, and without hesitation he said—and I quote, "homosexuality." That was it. That was the unpardonable sin. I could feel the blood run out of my face and I just sat there cold and dead. The logical part of me knew better, but still, there it was, a strange sense of despair washing over me.

Edina grabbed me right after the service and asked me how I was doing. I told her fine, but she invited me to come over to the house immediately so that we could talk. On the pretense of having a get-together she invited several people over and I was one of them. Then as soon as everybody began mingling, she found a place where we could go and talk privately. And I started crying. I knew in my head that I hadn't committed the unpardonable sin, but I also felt in my heart that I would never be of any use to God until I got rid of this homosexuality. And while it might not have been the unpardonable sin, it was still a very significant sin; one with no release.

After that, and a couple of other similar episodes, I decided that I wasn't going to be spending a lot of time in that church anymore either. And at this time I was getting frustrated with God. How could I serve him fully if he would not help me with this problem? And why wouldn't he help me? He was the one who had the problem with it. If he had just left it alone, then I would be okay. And how could I be responsible for a "sin" over which I had no control? It was as if God had taken this "emotion," put it inside of me, turned it up to the highest level he could, and then said... "Oh, by the way, you can't use it!"

I continued to pray and to seek God. And my writing reflected that. I continued to go deeper and my music seemed to get more and more sincere. I found that people responded to it even more deeply in Cody than they did in Riverton. There was no question that I was connected with God, but when it came to the issue of my sexuality, he seemed unmoved. And I always felt that until this was gone, there would be no "ultimate" connection that I was seeking.

After about a year in Cody, my mom was again transferred through her work. This time she was transferred to Billings, Montana. This was a welcome change for me because at least Billings had a population over one-hundred thousand people. I was ready for the "Big City."

In Billings I heard about a big church called the First Assembly of God Church. I was a little uneasy about it because it was a little too charismatic, but I gave it a try. It turned out that I liked it okay. The music was great, and I had a wonderful time and met some wonderful people.

While in Billings I started doing something that I really loved but didn't do a lot of in Riverton or Cody. I started acting. Well you know what that means. Of course at that time I hadn't really made those associations (actors are gay). Once again, I was pretty sheltered with my small town acumen. I managed to land a small role in the musical Jesus Christ Superstar.

After the play closed, I went to the cast party. That was a lot of fun. There was one guy there who I thought was absolutely gorgeous. I had been trying to ignore those feelings during the play when we had struck up a conversation or two. That night after the cast party he offered to take me home. I took him up on it since I didn't have a car, and it would be faster than walking. He asked if he could stop by his house first to pick something up, and I said fine. By now it was almost morning and I was really tired from partying all night.

On the way to the house we played the questions game. Where are you from? What do want to be when you grow up? What's your favorite Andrew Lloyd Webber musical? As we drove along though, his questions got more personal. Then he said, as if he was aware that I may be getting uncomfortable, "Ask me anything you want to know about me." We walked into the house and sat down and started talking. Again he asked me the same question. I didn't know what to ask, so I said "What is it you want me to ask?" He looked at me very carefully and said "Do you want to take a shower?" Of course it was now daylight, I had been partying all night, and I was starting to feel the effects of it, so I wasn't quite firing on all thrusters. I asked him "Why, do I stink." That embarrassed him, and suddenly I realized what he was talking about.

I looked at his face. He was beautiful. After a moment of silence, I told him yes, and we got into the shower. While I was with him I was in ecstasy. We finished with the shower and went to bed. Lying next to him felt right to me. We lay there for several minutes in each other's arms, and to be honest I didn't want to ever move again. With those thoughts in mind, I fell asleep and didn't awake up for several hours.

We went out a few times, but I was overcome with guilt and fear that someone in my church would find out, and I finally told him what I was going through. He didn't understand, but that didn't matter. I had to do what I thought was right. So that was the end of that relationship, my third "relationship" really to speak of.

Even though I did what I thought was right, I was angry, lonely and frustrated. I was angry with God. So I rattled off my mantra. "Why won't He help me?" So in a rather visible way, I lashed out at God. Some of my friends were worried, but there was no way I could really tell them what was going on inside of my head.

I decided to take a huge risk, and I went and talked to one of the associate pastors of the church. I told him about my struggle and told him that I didn't know what to do. He recommended that I go to a therapist, and gave me the name of one who attended the church. So I was now on my second therapist, my third counselor.

Despite all the time I spent with him, I never felt that we were making any progress. He tried praying with me, talking to me, anointing me with oil, casting demons out of me, and all manner of other things that he thought would work, but they didn't. At his advice I tried a technique which I believe he called "aversion therapy." With this therapy, every time I thought about a man, I would sniff this chemical. It stank. It was the foulest odor I had ever smelled. His explanation was that my brain would replace the pleasure of the fantasy, with the pain from the odor. I thought it would work, so I did this dutifully for several months while I saw him.

After Jesus Christ Superstar, I got hooked up with a comedy troop known as "Actors and Other Diseases." They were an improvisational group doing material very similar to the popular TV show hosted by Drew Carrey, "Who's Line is it Anyway?" I was originally invited to join the group because I was a writer and the coach thought I could help come up with scenarios and scenes, but we soon discovered that I could improv with the best of them. I was very happy there, but I found myself compromising in so many ways. I had made a promise to God that I would always be true to Him no matter what, but it soon got to the point that I would do just about anything for a laugh. I was highly successful in this group, but I was at odds with what I believed about God.

After about a year in Billings, I got a little stir crazy and wanted to move on to greener pastures. I had an aunt in Seattle, Washington, and so I called and asked 'if I was able to save up some money, could I stay with her for a while?' Knowing that it wasn't very likely that I would raise a lot of money in Billings, my aunt invited me to come out anyway, and not to worry about the expense. So I moved out to Seattle.

The irony of this story as that soon after I left Billings, I learned that the associate pastor I had gone to in Billings to seek advice—his son had recently come out to his family and friends. I don't know how they all handled that, but I had met this boy. He was about my age, and there wasn't any doubt in my mind that he was gay. But I just figured he was working on his own issues too.

SEATTLE

The first few weeks in Seattle were the most difficult. I didn't know anyone; I didn't have a job, spending money, a car, a friend, or even a driver's license. One day my aunt dropped me off at a place called the "Dance of Joy." This was a place where they played music that Christians could dance to in an environment where Christians could hang out without the other trappings of the nightlife. I sat in this place of about two hundred people and felt totally alone. Everyone around me was having fun, and dancing, and sipping their mocktails, and laughing and sweating and talking to one another.

To get to know people, I had tried a couple of the larger churches in the area, but they were cold and very unfriendly. I would have had better luck trying to make friends with a polar bear than to get even a response from these people. I tried out for the choir in one such church, and they wanted me to sign a contract stating that I would attend rehearsals, and the performances for at least one year. That freaked me out. It reminded me of some of the tactics the pastors in Riverton had used to manipulate their parishioners to do their bidding.

Outside of this dance hall there was a hill, and up on the hill were several trees and bushes. I went up there where I could be alone and just think. While I was up there I had what I have termed a "raw" conversation with God. That was a conversation in which I was honest about how I felt, and I didn't couch it in flowery or religious words. I talked with him honestly about my frustration, my loneliness, about the challenges I was facing at that time. Since my aunt had dropped me off, I couldn't' just leave. I had to wait until the time we had decided that she would pick me up. So I was stuck there. And that made me angrier, and as I got angrier, I had more to say about it to God.

"Dammit God!" I shouted into the air. "You know full well that I have not only been eager, but that it's been my total desire to serve you with all my heart. So why can't you accept that? Either accept me or reject me, but stop toying with me. Dammit!"

After the conversation, I went down and sat on the steps of the building. I made a vow that if anyone started talking to me about Jesus; I was going to let them have it. For the moment, I was not a Christian (I knew that would change once I calmed down, but for now I was just too worked up), and I was ready to do battle against God if need be.

While I was sitting there, a guy came out and sat beside me. He sat there for a couple of minutes, and then he turned to me and held out his hand. "I'm Tom" he said, and we shook. I was in shock. It had only been five minutes since my conversation with God, and already somebody was talking to me. I told Tom that I was new to Seattle, and didn't know a lot of people, and that I was looking for a church.

Tom told me about the church he went to, and then told me he had a friend who lived in my area and could pick me up that Sunday morning. Tom seemed nice, so I decided I would check it out.

So Tom's friend showed up that Sunday morning and took me to church. This was a large church of about 5,000 members called Eastside Foursquare Church. The basic philosophy of Eastside was pretty simple. They were interested in creating a healthy church with healthy members who could think for themselves. They trusted me with my relationship with God and unlike any of the churches I had attended in the past; they didn't tell me how to think (or even how to vote for that matter). And should I want to join any of their volunteer ministries, I would not be required to sign a contract.

My first day there, the pastor told the congregation how God had instructed him to give away something that he considered valuable, and how he argued with God before finally giving in. He did it, and he still didn't feel great about it, but he was happy that he had been obedient to God. He was honest and vulnerable as a pastor, and this was a church that I could feel safe in.

As time went on, I met a lot of people who liked to sharpen their "spiritual" skills on one another through discussion and banter, though it was rarely personal. I would spend over fourteen years in this church, and from the day I walked in, it was my home.

Thanks to my involvement in the church and my large group of friends, I managed to "control" my thoughts (well, at least my actions) for about two years. I worked hard keeping that beach ball under the water without drawing attention to myself. But sure enough, it began to surface again. When it did, it picked the worst time (don't they always?). Or perchance it was all the other circumstances that brought it out, I don't know. Aside from my aunt, the rest of my family was in Montana. My mom and sister were in Billings, and my grandparents were in Kalispell/Summers. My grandfather was diabetic, and the disease was taking its toll on his body. I received a call one day at work from my sister informing me that my grandfather had had a heart attack, and died.

This hit me very hard. It was his third heart attack in just as many years. During those other heart attacks, I was able to get to Kalispell and sit with him while he recovered. While I was there we didn't talk much, but I would sit by his bed for long periods of time. I think this was healing for us. There were many times as I was sitting there chatting with him, that I wondered if I shouldn't have offered at least some explanation as to why I was so troubled when I was a teenager, but I decided that it might not be good for his heart. But now I would never be able to tell him how much it meant to me that he stepped in and try to help out his grandson.

Shortly after hearing about my grandfather's death, I got word that I would be losing my job, and that my roommates were moving out. I was living in an apartment with two other guys, both people I had met through church. The two of them were moving into a big house with a friend of theirs, and I was "uninvited." All these things came together to create what was about to become a pivotal point in my life, and in my relationship with God.

I was approaching the end of my endurance. I was becoming anxious and the struggle seemed to me to be getting out of control. Alone in my living room, with tears and frustration, I told God that I was not going last much longer. Later that night I sat alone in the dark weeping. I tried to find some music on the radio that might lift me up. While flipping through the channels with the remote, I happened to pass the Christian radio station, and even though I rarely ever listened to it because the music was too mellow, and too cheesy, I decided I would leave it there. Perhaps it would cheer me up. While I was listening, I heard an ad for an organization called Metanoia Ministries. They specialized in working with homosexuals who wanted to live their lives for Christ.

Metanoia was a part of an organization called Exodus International, and their whole purpose on the planet was to lead the homosexual out of his sins and into a Biblical sexuality. They offered programs, counseling, classes, and other forms of reparative therapy to help get the Christian into a right relationship with Christ. So the next morning I called them. They told me their location, and asked me to come in for an interview. We talked at length about my struggle, and the counselor took me into the lobby and gave me a whole bunch of literature on the subject for me to read. The therapy was based on a sliding scale (after all, if you're going to try to live the Biblical lifestyle you're going to have to pay for it). The problem was: this wasn't covered by insurance. Blue Cross just didn't care that I was gay. Of course, being unemployed, I didn't have access to insurance.

I worked hard in this group and never missed a session. Okay, I did miss one. I was living in the suburbs at the time, and I was early for my appointment, so I found myself downtown in Seattle (I didn't go downtown much because I was afraid that it would lead me into sin). While I was exploring the downtown area, I came across an adult bookstore, and I went in. This was the first time I had been in one of these, and as soon as I walked in I could feel the blood rushing to my head (both of them). My breathing became tight, and I was so almost numb from the fear, the excitement, and the lack of oxygen. I bought a magazine and a toy and immediately went home to play with it. I called up my counselor and told him that my back had gone out (I was in a severe car accident in 1987, and to this day I have some pretty serious back problems because of it). He believed me, and I rescheduled for next week. That appointment I did keep and every one after that.

Along with the counseling sessions, they were offering a class called Living Waters, and I signed up for that too. This class was intensive, and would take the student through the process of healing, culminating in the Healing Prayer that was so popular in the early nineties thanks to Leanne Payne. We were each given workbooks, and put into small groups with a leader, and then held accountable to each other to work through our issues. I spent several months in this class until it was finished, and then I joined a support group.

PORN

My first true exposure to porn would have to be the underwear section of the Sears catalog in the early 80s. After that I discovered a couple of magazines, such as Men's Fitness and Men's Health. Later I would stumble onto a magazine called International Male. The bodies in these magazines were so beautiful, and the clothes that they wore looked so nice on them.

I once stumbled across a Penthouse or a Hustler magazine (I think I found it in a garbage can), and I kept it hidden under my bed in my room. This had girls in it, but it also had guys. Once my friend Connie bought a copy of Playgirl, and when nobody was looking she let me borrow it. I was so excited. This was pretty much my first exposure to a naked man (remember, this is the early eighties, and the internet didn't exist yet). But I never hung on to these things for fear that someone would find out about me and I was worried that I was hanging onto something that would lead me into sin. This was true in Riverton, Cody, Billings, and Seattle.

It was in Seattle that I discovered "Men's Fitness," "Exercise for Men Only," and "Men's Health." I wouldn't subscribe to these magazines because I was afraid that I would be giving in to my sinful urge, so instead I just bought the magazine every month when it came out. I was, at the time, starting a new workout regiment, so nobody would suspect anything of it (or they never voiced it anyway).

My first exposure to hard-core gay porn was that day in downtown Seattle, and I was determined not to let it get to me. So after a few weeks of owning the magazines, I burned them in my fireplace as a sacrifice unto the Lord and as a sign of my repentance.

At this point I was dating Sonya. Sonya was a beautiful blonde that I met at church and we had so much in common. I liked her a lot, and I thought that this time my relationship could be blessed by God. We dated for a while until it became obvious that I wasn't able to be there physically. I could hug, kiss, and cuddle, but somehow it showed that I wasn't really into it even though I made the extra effort to be cuddly and attentive.

While Sonya and I were dating, I met Alex. I don't remember how we met; only that it was through church. Alex looked like Charlie Sheen. We all three would hang out together, and I couldn't ignore the fact that I really wanted Alex more than I wanted Sonya. Sonya knew that something was wrong, and we began to fight. So in order to keep from hurting her anymore, I came clean with her about what I was going through. Oddly enough she was very understanding, and she told me that she would help me work it out.

So now we were dating with full disclosure.

It was during this time that I ended up in the adult bookstore. After a few weeks I told her about it, and she tried to be sympathetic, but she told me that she was so disappointed with me. To be honest, I couldn't blame her. So to prove to her (and to God) that I was serious, I grabbed up my collection of Men's Fitness and other "health" magazines, and I threw them into the fire. Now there was nothing between us.

But I still couldn't be there for Sonya the way she needed me to be there, and we broke up. Oddly enough, this was very troubling to me. I don't really know if it was because I truly loved her, or it was that I failed yet again. It was probably a little bit of both. I was no closer healing now than when I first started.

PALMTREE

Shortly after that, I took a job as an actor with a Christian theater company called PalmTree Theater. At first it seemed like a dream job. I was going to be an actor, traveling around the Northwest United States, and I was going to be doing a job that really made a difference in the world around me. We did three plays that dealt with substance abuse and family dysfunction, both issues near and dear to my heart. Each one of these plays was geared for different ages. One play was written specifically to grade school age children, one geared for Jr. High School students, and the third geared toward High School and College age students. It was an eye-opening job on many levels.

On the one hand, the kids looked up to us. There's something about putting someone on stage that creates an instant connection and instant trust. Because I was on the stage, and because I was portraying something so powerful and close to most of these kids' experience, they trusted me (I usually played the heavy, the drug dealers and users). After just about every show several young people would come up to talk and they would talk about how their own lives seemed to mirror what they saw on stage. These were things they couldn't talk about with their friends and especially their teachers, so they talked to me about it. I felt like I was on the front lines of a major war and I was looking at so many casualties and I didn't know how to respond.

I listened to other members of the group shell out advice, which was "right out of the Bible" (albeit couched in a modern language). But it did little to help these kids. I think it was here that I began to realize how much the so-called Christian ethic didn't, and wouldn't work in real life situations. So I started asking myself why. And what could I say to these kids that would help them through some of these hideous events?

PalmTree consisted of the founders of the theater, Matthew and his wife, and Trevor and his wife. Matthew and Trevor were the directors, and they decided which plays were produced and then cast them and directed them. The only other person on staff was Flora, who handled the box office and other office administration affairs. During productions they would contract with other people to design their sets and take care of production issues. They didn't pay any of their actors except the Road Company. That was me.

The Road Company was just that. That part of PalmTree that took to the road. We traveled from town to town throughout the Northwest, performing to schools and church groups. When we performed, we stayed with host families who sometimes put us all up together, or sometimes separated us. There were five of us on the Road Company, three girls and two guys. Candice was the Road Company manager and occasionally filled in as an actor when needed. It was her job to deal with all the administration issues on the road (and while on the road, she was our boss). Then there were the four of us, two girls and two guys. We got along okay, but as with any group of people, we had problems. The irony about this group is that the two guys were gay, and one of the girls was a lesbian. We didn't know it at first, but as time went on—I never admitted what I was going through to anyone because I was afraid of what the consequences might be, both at PalmTree, and in my church. I was also "believing" for God's healing, so I refused to wear the label gay. Instead, I pretended to be straight, telling myself that I was "a new creature in Christ Jesus, and "living as if..."

Because it was common to separate the guys from the girls, Jeff and I spent a lot of time together. During this time we talked about a lot of things, and Jeff hinted that he was going through something. He would talk about this "issue" he was going through. As I listened to him, his words became oddly familiar. So one day, when the two of us were alone, I asked Jeff, "Are you struggling with homosexuality?"

Jeff told me no, that he wasn't "struggling" with it.

So I asked him, "Are you gay?"

He said yes, but that he wasn't going to try to change. He couldn't.

I never told Jeff about my own struggle, even though this would have been the perfect time. This was partly because he had decided not to fight and just accept that this was who he was (he was letting go of the beach ball), and I didn't want to accept that he could do this and still be a Christian (or worse, that he could be right).

At PalmTree, I somehow became a lightening rod and there were a lot of very bad feelings. PalmTree considered itself to be liberal, but in reality they were only liberal compared to Ann Coulter or Rush Limbaugh. At Eastside I had never thought too much about politics. I voted, and was involved in political issues, but Eastside didn't espouse any political views, and they weren't very tolerant of people that pushed their views on others. They were there to find God, and everything else was that person's choice. So I never considered myself a liberal. As a matter of fact, that particular election I voted for George Bush Senior.

When I took the job with PalmTree, I became painfully aware that I was, in fact, very liberal. But I wasn't just politically liberal, I was also liberal in the area of spirituality and Christianity, and I was chastised on an almost daily because of my spiritual views. Sometimes, during our Bible Study/Touch In, without thinking I would weigh in on my spiritual view regarding whatever issue we were talking about. I remember one day I mentioned that I didn't like Solomon. I felt that God had given him so much, money and wisdom, and influence, and yet he never really used all that wisdom for the good of his country; and he was horrible to his people. At that moment Matthew, the owner, informed me that I had no right to feel that way because Solomon wrote the Bible. I pointed out that Solomon enslaved his own people and indentured them so that he could build a temple to God. I also pointed out that when his own son ascended to the throne, the Israelites asked him not to be like his father. And when he refused, that's when Israel split into Judah and Israel.

Then there was the topic of money. Once I was talking about money, and I just happened to mention that Jesus spoke more on the issue of money than he did on any other subject.

"Not according to my Bible" Marcy chided (Marcy was one of the members of the road company).

"Maybe you've just been reading the wrong Bible" I fired back.

So that turned into a big fight. But strangely enough, the next day an article turned up by a guy named Larry Burkett in which he pointed out that, in fact, "Jesus spoke more on the topic of money than on any other topic in the Bible." But I wasn't vindicated because they all looked away from me when they read it, and they never brought the subject up again.

I knew that Jeff and Janice (the other two actors) were more liberal, but they didn't talk about it. I guess they were smart and learned their lesson from me. We would sometimes joke about how liberal Marcy and Candice thought they were, but that was always between us.

PalmTree represented Christianity's true feelings toward a lot of things, and the strongest was homosexuality. There wasn't a day that passed without some derisive comment toward the homosexuals. This became harder and harder for me to take. After a while I did what I usually do when I get upset. I said something.

Previously that week, there had been a march for gay rights in the Seattle area. Trevor was going on at length about the position this put our city in spiritually. He continued to "worry" that we were bringing our city closer to God's wrath.

We were all sitting there working on some fliers and mailers, and I lost myself in the frustration.

"I think God would be okay with giving his children basic human rights, even if they didn't see eye to eye with God."

Jeff and Janice looked at me. I could tell they were glad I said it, but the next thing I know I was soundly "rebuked in the Name of Jesus." Trevor quoted scripture at me and informed me that it was attitudes like mine that only brought this city closer to God's wrath. Then he went off on a tirade.

"This is the church's fault" he kept repeating. "We should never have allowed this happen. We have abandoned God's command, and I take the blame."

Aside from being a drama queen, I felt that this man was trying to pretend he had "love" but in reality he was spitting hate. Jeff and Janice and I were just angry. Jeff thought it was just because I was sensitive to his issues, but I was also well aware of Trevor's feelings toward me as well.

Later that year a Family Values group decided to hold a Christian Family Values rally, and they chose Volunteer Park in Seattle as their location. There are thousands of parks in the city of Seattle, but they chose to hold this rally in the only park in the city that is frequented almost exclusively by gay and lesbian; and gay and lesbian friendly people. Needless to say, there was a massive protest by gay rights activists.

For the next two months this event was all I heard about. Trevor and Matthew and Candice went on and on regarding how they had been attacked simply because they represented Christian Family Values and that Satan himself was trying to destroy the family using these groups. The fact that they could have had this rally at any other park didn't even cross their minds. The fact that they had done nothing but instigate problems with the gay community meant nothing. To them, all they saw was their own righteous indignation. Just about every radio station in town was talking about this event, and they all agreed on one thing. This gathering should have happened somewhere else, but it appeared that the Christians wanted to start a fight.

KYLE MARTIN

One night the Road Company did a show for a Seventh-Day-Adventist academy in a suburb south of Seattle. It was so weird and frightening for me to be back at an academy so close to the one I went to in Colorado.

We arrived on campus early in the afternoon, and our show was that evening, so I had several hours to think back on my experience at Campion. The more I thought about it, the more troubled I became. Tony's comment, "Faggot," being kicked out, trying to hide my beach ball, all those memories came rushing back. I was miserable, and the others thought I was just being melodramatic. So I went off into a corner to pout, and to try to console myself (and yes, wallow in some melodrama).

During the show, I had a panic attack in the middle of one of my scenes, and nearly wasn't able to finish. I was afraid I would have to leave the stage. This wasn't the first time I had ever had a panic attack, but this was one of the worst (and most inconvenient) times. At this point though, I did not know what a panic attack was. We hadn't discussed those in therapy. I suddenly went numb all throughout my body, and I got a strange sensation that I was going to pass out on stage or forget my lines and that I was going to freak out in front of all these people. My chest tightened and I could hardly breathe. I wanted to run off stage and hide before things got out of control.

I didn't do any of those things though. I sat there and focused all my energy on Janice's face and ran my lines mechanically until I could calm down. I was scared to death, and it turns out I scared everyone else too. They could all see it on my face that something was definitely wrong. They could see the terror in my eyes, and now they were worried about me. After the show, they asked me how I was doing, and I had a brief chance to tell them of my previous experiences with a Seventh-Day-Adventist school, carefully omitting the story of Tony and his remark of course. After the show many of the students and faculty came up and talked to us. They were very generous, and I was in a much better place than I had been in Campion.

A few weeks later I was channel surfing, and I heard one of those television evangelists talking about demon oppression versus demon possession. Needless to say, my ears perked up considering my recent attack on stage. So I listened to him. He explained that while Satan could not actively possess a Christian, he could oppress them. Normally I would have been skeptical, but in light of my own panic attack (and since I didn't know it was a panic attack), I was more than willing to entertain the idea.

Eastside Foursquare Church had a large singles group at the time, and they met every Friday night. I looked forward to those Friday nights when I was in town and could attend the services. Our singles pastor was also the associate pastor, and he was a man I considered to be trustworthy and respectable. He was also funny and a darn good speaker.

I had been at Eastside and very involved in the church for many years now, so Kyle Martin knew who I was. After a Friday night service I approached him. My plan was to simply ask him a question and see what his response was. I asked him if he believed that Christians could be oppressed by the Devil.

"The short answer is 'Yes,'" he said. Then he briefly explained the difference.

I was satisfied with his answer, but he asked me to stick around for a minute. He quickly finished up his conversations with those around him, and took me into another room behind the stage and we talked. He wanted to know what was going on, so I told him about my bizarre experience on the stage during my performance.

After a rather lengthy talk we concluded that it was just a panic attack. He explained to me what they were and I was completely okay with that. Now that I knew what a panic attack was, I had a much better understanding of my experience. It also made sense to me, since my first experience with an Adventist academy was so traumatic. So I got up to leave, but he insisted that we pray together before I go.

While he was praying for me, he looked up at me and said, "I don't know if this is God, or the pizza, you decide, but I feel like God is saying to you, 'You're not gay.'"

I freaked out. Now the pastor knew, the pastor of a five-thousand member church. Now there was the potential for every one in my church to find out. My abilities to continue to be involved in the church were threatened; my job at PalmTree was threatened. But most importantly, my protective layers of secrecy were threatened. I was now vulnerable. In spite of my attempts to hide it, all I could do was cry. I had been struggling with this so long that once it was out in the open, it was like suddenly tearing the scab off an infected cut and letting all the puss drain out. I realize this is graphic, but that is just how it felt.

When it first happened, I was frustrated with God. How could he reveal such personal information about me to someone else, especially someone as potentially risky as Kyle Martin? But as I thought of this, something occurred to me. Maybe God told Kyle Martin because he knew that I needed to work through some of these feelings, and because he knew that he (actually, both God and I) could trust Kyle.

After a few hours, I felt my spirits lifting. Release had to be just around the corner. All those years, all that pain, all those memories, they were all about to culminate in the final wrap up where I was at last a heterosexual man who could love women; physically and emotionally. In my excitement, I stopped by a video store on the way home, and I rented a gay porn video.

I don't know why I rented the video. I think a lot of it had to do with the problems with PalmTree. I was preparing for a month long tour with them, and I just couldn't bear the thought of being in that environment for that long of time. That weekend I bought a case of beer, and I proceeded to get as drunk as I possibly could. I was fully aware of the irony of what I was doing; a guy who talked about and focused on alcohol abuse with thousands of students was now so drunk that he could barely walk.

Mickey and the Ex-Gay Groups

When the school year finally ended, that meant that my contract with PalmTree was over. I was never so glad to be away from any place than PalmTree. Emotionally I was a complete mess. I knew that deep down in my heart I really loved God and wanted to serve him completely, but PalmTree had made me feel like I was nothing but a rebellious reprobate and that I was, in fact, deceived into believing I was anything close to being a good Christian.

It took me several years to deal with these feelings and finally come to a place where I could say the name PalmTree without spewing angry venom. I know what you're going to ask, because everyone does. So let me tell you now—I have forgiven them. The reason I still talk about them as I do is that they still stand as a defining moment in my life when I saw Christianity's true colors.

Kyle Martin words haunted me for several more years. I had told very few people about them, but I held them in my mind for a long time. Around every corner I looked for my breakthrough to come. Around every corner I looked for God's power to break into my frailty, and to deliver me.

During this time, my relationship with God was still very good. I never let go of the hope that I would emerge from this struggle stronger and closer to him than I had ever been. But to help me facilitate this emergence, I elicited the help of more therapists.

On particular therapist kept calling everything that I told her "my fantasy" about life. So when she would talk to me, she would say, "In your fantasy of life..." this would happen, or "In your fantasy of life..." this is true, I got so angry with her for that. She was calling my pain fantasy, my thoughts fantasy, and I finally gave up and left her. I was paying her good money to dismiss all my feelings as fantasy.

One day Harvey Johnson, the head pastor of Eastside church spoke on the ways in which God spoke (and still speaks) to his people. In one point he told us that the best way to tell if someone was speaking for God was to wait and see if what they said came true.

It had been several years since my original conversation with Kyle Martin, so I decided that I would talk to Harvey. It was frightening to me, because that meant that now the head pastor of this mega-church would be in on my secret. But I needed to understand why healing wasn't forthcoming, especially since it was predicted by someone with the spiritual integrity of Kyle Martin. I explained to him what Kyle had said to me, and that I was still not seeing any evidence that things were turning around.

Harvey listened attentively, and then he introduced me to Mickey. Mickey was a member of Eastside who used to be gay many years ago, but now had overcome his sexuality and was successfully living his life as a heterosexual man. In fact, he was married and had two teenage boys and was now leading a group of his own into the new life of heterosexuality.

I met with Mickey at a local Starbucks and we had a long talk. I told him about what I was going through, and he listened. After our conversation, Mickey told me about his journey. He had made it. He was where I wanted to be. Mickey also ran an Exodus group: A group of men and women in all stages of finding their way out of the Deathstyle (what they called the homosexual lifestyle). So I went to my first Exodus meeting. There in front of all those guys, I tried to talk about how much I wanted to be free to serve God, and only ended up falling to pieces and embarrassing myself. But they seemed pretty accepting nonetheless.

I was part of Mickey's group for many years, and things went rather well. I started to feel better now that I had a support group that I could talk to. Life was good. Okay, I did almost drive my car off the road a couple times while staring at an ass that just wouldn't quit, but I kept telling myself that that was going to change as I continued to heal. As Mickey put it, we were "healing heterosexuals."

I spoke with two therapists at that time. One therapist, Reuben and I had some very candid talks about the issue of homosexuality. Reuben told me very carefully and very gently that he wasn't sure that there was anything that could be done to change the sexual orientation, and that instead of trying, I would be better off approaching my Christianity as a homosexual, and that I could apply all the rules about fidelity and morality within the confines of a homosexual relationship.

I liked Reuben a lot, but I wasn't yet ready to stop trying to change. I still believed that God wanted me to be straight, and I was determined that this would not come between us.

I also found another therapist who attended Eastside, and I used him to compliment my healing in Mickey's group. He also specialized in helping men who were trying to overcome their homosexuality. I talked with him for as long as my insurance would pay for it, which was about six months.

During that process, he told me that I needed to write a letter to my father calling him to account for his actions. I was reluctant to do so, but the therapist assured me that this was the best way for me to become stronger as a man. He told me about many of his other patients who had done the same thing and found themselves set free from their past. So I took him up on it, and I wrote the letter.

I told my father exactly how I felt about the way he treated me as a child. I told him honestly how I felt that he had abandoned me, and that I wondered why, after all these years, he hadn't made a single effort to even contact me.

My father wrote back. He was not happy with the letter, and he let me know in no uncertain terms. He told me that my letter gave him the idea that I wanted an apology, and that's the one thing I would never get from him. Needless to say, I didn't feel anything like my therapist said I would. But I wrote back one more time and told him that while it may be true, that I would never get that apology, a real man would be more than willing to acknowledge the wrong and harm he had caused another person. I told him that a real man would walk on his knees to make peace with the son he had so violently injured. But I accepted that as he was not capable of behaving like a real man.

That letter made me feel better, but it did not have the affect my therapist said it would. But before we could talk any more about it, my insurance ran out, and there wasn't any way I could pay the overwhelming amount of money that he wanted for therapy. So when we talked on our last day, his words to me were "Well, when you get the money, I'm here."

I was so angry to hear that. This wasn't just a little problem. To me it was spiritual life or death. I was trying to find a way to give my life totally to God, and all he cared about was the money. And he was a Christian. I left there feeling more discouraged than I had ever felt in my struggle so far. I went home and wept.

"What am I supposed to do?" I asked God. But there was no answer.

TINA

I met Tina through a group that I worked with called Radical for Jesus (I was their DJ). Radical for Jesus was a new incarnation of the Dance of Joy that I attended that first time in Seattle. Only now Radical for Jesus sponsored dances downtown Seattle and other gatherings for interfaith Christians. RFJ, as it was called, was highly successful at this point, and I enjoyed being part of it.

This particular time we were at a retreat sponsored by the group, and Tina was there. Tina was a fiery red-head with the most amazing personality of any woman I had ever met. She was beautiful, smart, compassionate, sincere, and she wanted nothing more in her life than to give it completely over to God. We were kindred spirits. And what was more, she liked me. We liked being around each other. We went on walks, we talked to each other, and we sometimes sat in silence just staring out at the beauty of the campsite around us. I remember one night we were sitting on a dock that overlooked a lake. It was late at night, and very dark. We talked somewhat, but mostly we just stared out into the sky and soaked in the incredible beauty. As we sat there, a shooting star so large it lit up most of the sky shot past us, its reflection in the water acting as a mirror making it look like they were coming toward each other. For nearly a minute we watched this, until at last it burned itself out. It was so beautiful and so amazing that we could barely catch our breath. I whispered into the night "Do it again daddy." It was so powerful. Maybe it was even a sign? Of all the girls I had ever met, Tina was the closest I had ever come to being in love. I really believed that it was possible that Tina could be the one for me.

As we spent more time with each other, I began to find myself more and more convinced that this was it. Tina was God's answer to me. I was finally going to be free. But again, I couldn't get intimate with her. I loved her mind, I loved her spirit, and quite frankly, her body was incredible too, but not to me. I loved her body the way most gay men love women's bodies. It was art. It was Van Gough, or Picasso, but it was something I would rather admire with my eyes, not with my hands. We got close emotionally, but not physically, and as I started experiencing the same frustration that I experienced with all those other girls, I just couldn't bring myself to go through it again. So I never told Tina anything, and we just stayed as friends. I never officially asked her to go out with me. Tina believed it was the man's duty to ask or to initiate the date, and that kind of let me off the hook. We could go all kinds of places together, Tina and I, but I didn't have to officially commit to a "date."

Tina was a good friend, and I tried so hard not to take advantage of her. So when she announced that she was dating a friend of mine, I again felt those same feelings of frustration, anger, and hopelessness. Again I felt like I was a failure. I said nothing. Eventually I was able to ask God to bless their relationship.

Brad

Brad was the son of one of the associate pastors at Eastside Church. At first the only thing we really had in common was that we were both musicians, more to the point, we loved to write music. And Brad wrote some really good music. As we met together, our friendship grew too. Brad was also very open about his sexuality. He was straight, but he didn't mind talking about sex and how he felt about it. This started to open up doors inside of me that I had never let open. I had never talked about sex as if it was a good thing. But Brad did, and he wasn't embarrassed about that.

Brad was also bothered by the fact that I didn't say too much about women. He couldn't figure out why. I continued to deny to him that I was gay, but in his mind if I wasn't chasing women, then I was. One night we were drinking and having fun. We had both had a lot to drink, and then Brad told me that he felt that there was a sexual tension between us. At first I didn't feel it, but when he said that I realized that there was something there. And I freaked out. We went for a walk outside and talked about it, and it was finally out in the open.

The next few months were difficult for me, because this was the first crush that I had ever had where the person I had the crush on actually knew how I felt. And he didn't really do anything to discourage it. I guess we kind of needed each other for whatever reason.

Another issue that Brad kind of hammered on was whether or not God really meant for me to be straight. He wasn't sure that I should be trying to go straight. In his mind he was wondering if we weren't just misunderstanding the issues around sexuality and maybe God created us as sexual beings and meant for us to behave as sexual beings. That was difficult for me to hear. I had invested years and years trying to turn myself around, and every time he suggested that I didn't need to try anymore, I felt a sense of despair well up inside me. But I couldn't get that nagging idea out of my head that he might be right. And if he was, then what was I going to do? Where would I turn? What would Mickey say?

My relationship with Brad was, to say the least, codependent; to say the most, honest. I had always been very proud of the fact that I was independent, and that I would never let anyone control me or make demands on me. This worked for all the women I dated, but it didn't work for Brad. Suddenly I wasn't so independent.

Brad's and my relationship went on like this for some time, until Brad took a job in Bellingham, Washington, about two hours north of Seattle. That little spot of time allowed me to recover from some of the codependence and confusion.

During that period of time I was asked to come and work for Eastside church, and I took the job gladly. But shortly after they hired me, Eastside fired me and I was starting to feel the pinch of dealing with them. I had only been working in this job for a few months, and they were not an easy church to work for. In fact, for the first time in my life, I was starting to feel that maybe it was time to move on. Maybe Eastside wasn't my home anymore.

My Way Out

At last I took a job contracting with the Microsoft Corporation. My job involved me going up on the internet and doing my research. I would go to random Web sites and look around, testing how accurate various search engines were. As a result, I was exposed to a lot of things that I had never been exposed to before. Some of the searches we did in these tests, while completely innocuous, returned some dicey pages. One such question we entered asked for information about grizzly bears. That's when I learned that a bear was a big hairy homosexual. Silly me, I had always thought it was a big, furry, four legged mammal that liked to eat fish and berries and hibernate in the winter.

While working at Microsoft, I was living in a house with two Born-Agains. I had been there about a year. Gene owned the house, and Larry and I were tenants. I was also volunteering at my church pretty extensively. I was writing sketches for the services, and I had directed two Christmas plays. One of the plays was so successful that the auditorium of twelve hundred seats was sold out every night.

Another of my other extracurricular activities was traveling with Mickey and his group to churches around the Seattle and outlying areas. Mickey was educating the church on the issues surrounding homosexuality. His goal was quite commendable. He was trying to create understanding of homosexuals, and to dissuade some of the passionate and angry emotions around the issue so that people in the churches today didn't have to go through what so many of us had gone through in our churches. So I wrote sketches and even performed in some of them to help the church understand what homosexuals went through in their journey to be the perfect cookie cutter Christian. I really enjoyed what I was doing. God was allowing me, finally, to live out my dream. Writing, performing, and traveling were my true love. And unlike PalmTree, I was accepted and supported as a Christian, and those around me considered me a conduit of wisdom, not a messenger from Satan or some Liberal reprobate.

Despite all this success, I was still struggling with those extreme emotions. My beach ball wanted to surface. The only way to describe these intense feelings to you would be to say "starve yourself for a week or two, and then go into a grocery store." That was the power of these emotions, and it was getting harder and harder to suppress them.

One day during lunch at Microsoft, I decided to go up on the internet and research gay bars in the Seattle area. (I should point out that this was not illegal, as I wasn't surfing for porn, I was merely looking for established businesses. Although because of the nature of my job, if we stumbled across porn while doing our research, we logged it into the database and treated it as any other search.) At the time of my search I only found a couple, so I checked them out just to see what they were like. At one bar I met a guy who introduced me to the bathhouses in Seattle. At the bathhouse, I could have sex with anyone who wanted to. It was easy. You took off all your clothes and walked around in a towel. Then other guys would pass you, and if they were interested they would give you a look. If you looked back, then you were hooked up.

This was my first time with a man in a very long time, and it was amazing. During the whole time I was there I was in ecstasy. I used the opportunities to experience all those things I had thought about in my fantasies, but had never tried. I ran my hands up and down the bodies, I experienced the closeness to them, and I felt free. I left the bathhouse and went home. I felt so free and so close to someone for the first time in my life. But that freedom soon changed to guilt. The next day I felt so guilty I went over to Mickey's house and through many tears told him what had happened. Then I cried and "repented" and the two of us prayed together.

I was still writing sketches for Eastside and sometimes actually performing in them, though I felt somewhat the hypocrite for doing so. For the next few months I stayed "straight" and avoided downtown Seattle at all cost. But I couldn't get the memory of those men out of my head. So I went out one Friday night to a bar just to hang out and see what it was like. I was new to the scene, so I didn't do much but observe. But there was something really powerful about watching these men show affection toward each other. It was something I had never seen except in the videos I rented, and that wasn't really affection, it was just bad acting. But to watch this happen in front of me was amazing.

They were so free, so open. They didn't have to hide from anyone. Their beach balls were on top of the water. I don't know what happened to me that night, but I couldn't get it out of my head how nice it must feel to just be myself. I think the beach ball had finally gotten the better of me and despite all my efforts otherwise, it had surfaced.

Before long, I signed up for an internet dating service, and through that I met a few people. I even joined a baseball team for the gay league. It was like having a new family, and I was loving life. All my Christian friends were impressed that I was doing something that involved sports. Even Tina couldn't stop saying how proud she was of me. But I never told them which league I was on.

The new millennium was now upon us, and while everybody around me worried about the Y2K bug, I worried about where my life was going to go from there. Now that I was experimenting, what did that mean? Would I keep trying to change, or would I just give up. I was truly on the verge of a major decision. One Friday night I went out to my favorite bar, and I had a little too much to drink. I didn't really want to drive home so I decided to spend the night at a bathhouse. Of course when I tell my friends that this was why I was at the bathhouse, they all look at me and nod in a sort of "if that's what you want us to believe, that's what we'll pretend we believe" sort of way. Another thing that made the bathhouse so attractive was that I had just come out, and so I didn't know anyone. This was a way to experience that connection or experience I had been longing for.

The next night, Saturday night, my sister, Rachel, who was by now a flight attendant for American Airlines, came into town. So I went to visit her along with several of my friends from church. We all had a fun time and stayed up late. I had to go home a little early because I had a ball game on Sunday morning. Sunday afternoon the teams were invited to one of the local bars to get together and celebrate the games. At the bar I met somebody who wanted to take me home with him. We had a great time, and I ended up spending the night at his place. The next morning, on Monday, I went home before work to take a shower and change my clothes.

When I got home I found a note on my pillow from my roommate which read "Ben, the police were here asking some very serious questions… What's going on Ben?" Attached to the note was a card from a police officer, and below that was his title and division. "Detective… Homicide." Well immediately I became concerned because I thought that someone I had met on Friday night must have been killed. So I picked up the phone and called the number on the card.

The first thing the detective said to me was that he wanted to know what was going on at the club over the weekend, and why I didn't stick around when my partner went into convulsions. This confused me because I never saw anyone go into convulsions. I told the officer that, and he become a little irritated.

"You're not in any trouble" he kept reiterating, "I just want to know what happened."

"I don't know what you're talking about" I told the detective.

"Look, the guy died and we want to know why."

"If someone had died next to me then I think I would have remembered it."

"We have proof that you were there."

"I'm not denying that I was there, but nobody died when I was there. At least not that I knew of."

"You're not in any trouble, we just need the truth."

"And I'm telling you the truth."

The argument went on for over a half-hour. Finally, he said "Look, we have it on video surveillance tape."

So I said "I'm coming down to the station right now, and I want to see this tape." I asked for his address and told him that it would take me about fifteen or twenty minutes to get downtown.

He backed off a little bit at that point and we started talking again.

As it turned out, the guy they were talking about died on Saturday night, the night I was with my sister and our friends, not on Friday night, the night I was actually at the club. But the damage was done. The police had visited the Born-Agains, and I was officially "outed."

That massive decision I was on the brink of making had been made for me.

This was a very difficult time for me. The first thing I had to do was sit down with my roommate, the one who owned the house, and talk with him. Gene told me that he was really quite surprised and that he didn't know what to do. He was also a friend of Tina's (though he met her through me), and because he was so freaked out, he went over to her house and asked her if she knew anything about my personal lifestyle. Well she didn't, and she was as surprised as he was. But that certainly explained a lot that had happened between us.

Tina and I hadn't talked in a while, but I suddenly got a message on my voice-mail from her, asking how I was doing. I knew then that Gene must have talked to her, but I also knew Tina, and I knew that she was concerned about me. She was fully aware that I was about to embark on a very difficult journey, and she wanted to be there for me. That meant more to me I think than anything that had happened between us up to that point.

It turned out that the Born Agains didn't want me living with them anymore. They were just too freaked out. Even if I was planning on "repenting" and going straight, they couldn't handle it. So I would be looking for a new place to live. My contract with the Microsoft Corporation was up that month as well, and so I would be looking for another job and another place to live, both at the same time. On top of that, I had to leave my church. They weren't about to let me continue writing for them or performing, and I couldn't handle all the whispering. Remember, this was a big church, and I was fairly visible there, so I disappeared.

All this happened around mother's day, 2000. This meant that I had to take my mother to dinner, and tell her why I was coming out after all this time, although coming out was never my plan. After having spent fifteen years trying to drown my beach ball, I was experimenting with what it might be like to let the beach ball surface. Thanks to the police though, I was coming out in a way that wouldn't allow me to go back into the closet.

We went to my mom's favorite restaurant. We talked briefly about what had just happened, and then she told me that she wanted to talk about it in a more private place so that she could cry. That was the last thing I needed to hear. I told her that if she needed to cry, then I couldn't talk. It was simply too much for me.

She had brought her little New Testament and wanted to read to me a couple of scriptures.

"Do you think I haven't researched this?" I asked her.

Her response was "Humor me."

So I listened to her read her scriptures, one out of Romans, and the other out of Corinthians. She got to Corinthians, where Paul said, "Neither the sexually immoral nor idolaters nor adulterers nor male prostitutes nor homosexual offenders..." I pointed out another part of the scripture further down which she hadn't noticed, "And that is what some of you were."

After having read that, she couldn't understand why I wouldn't keep trying. But I was through trying. Fifteen years was enough. And now that my proclivities had been proclaimed upon the rooftops, I may as well take advantage of the freedom that had been offered to me.

Soon after that I talked to my sister on the phone. She believed that my decision to stop trying to change meant that she would never see me again after this lifetime. I'll never forget the comment she made to me while talking on the phone... "But I don't want you to go to Hell."

At first I laughed, and that offended her. But I didn't care. She had no idea how offensive this was to me. So I asked her, "How do you think I feel? You're telling me that I'm going to hell."

The next few weeks were tumultuous ones. I got a letter from Mickey in e-mail officially asking me to leave Exodus. But he was sure to include a statement saying that as soon as I wanted to get things right with Jesus, I would be welcome there again.

Through a strange coincidence I ran into a guy I used to work with at Microsoft at one of the bars I started to frequent. We worked in the same group, but in different offices, and so we never really talked to each other, but we knew who each other was. When he saw me at the bar, he was very surprised. He had no idea. I told him about what had recently transpired, and he just happened to be looking for a roommate in the Capitol Hill area of Seattle (that's where all the bars and such are located). This was perfect for me because it put me where the action was. I was now within staggering distance from the clubs. The next few weeks were spent moving, job hunting, moving out of my office at Microsoft, getting resettled in my new apartment and job hunting some more, wondering if anyone from my church was going to at least call me and see how I was, job hunting, wondering if anyone from Exodus was going to call and check in on me, job hunting, and job hunting some more.

In the midst of all this I called my friend Corey, and asked if we could get together for lunch. Corey is one of those friends that I have cherished for a very long time, and we got together and chatted. The first thing that Corey said to me was that although he didn't understand, he knew me, and he knew that I had given this decision a lot of thought. It was a quiet, off-the-cuff statement, but it meant a lot to me. He was the first person to actually say that he knew me, and he trusted that I had given this decision a lot of attention.

He was right. I had been thinking about this decision for months/ years before I actually made it. While it seemed as if it just happened all of a sudden, the truth was, it took years to get me to the point where I could have been able to make the decisions I made and live with the consequences that followed.

There's so much more to this story that I don't know if I could tell it without bogging it down, but these events all brought me here to this point, where I could leave "my closet" without feeling guilty and without fear.

SEPTEMBER 11, 2001

My sister Rachel was a flight attendant for American Airlines during the process of my transition. While she lived in Fort Worth, Texas, she wasn't able to talk to me except over the phone. My transition was tough on her too. I think a lot of it had to do with our Christian upbringing. In her mind, there was the possibility that I was going to hell. But there was something else. Being a flight attendant, she had more dealings with gay men than she wanted to. I think that being a flight attendant is very similar to being an actor. In order to qualify for either, you've got to be gay. (It's in the gay membership handbook.)

When she first graduated from her flight attendant classes, American sent her to Boston. It was there that she met her friend

Jeff. She and Jeff were pretty close, and they stayed close even after she moved to Dallas. The nice thing about being a flight attendant is the mobility, and so Rachel and Jeff could stay in touch and visit each other often.

When I came out, it was in Jeff that she found her greatest comfort. Jeff wasn't her brother, he was an unbiased observer. He could walk with her through this transition, and he took great pains to help her understand where I was coming from. All in all, he was one of her best friends during that time. I met Jeff once when I visited Rachel in Boston, but I was still hiding out in closets at that time, so I pretended I was straight and we didn't talk too much.

I met my partner in February, 2001. I was shopping at a local mall up on Capitol Hill, and as I walked toward the bathroom, he walked past me. He was gorgeous, and what a body. But I was very shy, and I didn't say anything to him. We looked at each other as we walked through the mall, but that's about as far as it got. I figured it was fun flirting.

About two nights later I went to a video store in that mall, and he was there looking at videos with a friend of his. So I watched him slightly, but still I never said anything. I found a video just after he found a video, and I ended up in line just behind him. As I was standing in line he made a joke to his friend. He was talking about business cards, and he said "everybody has business cards." And to prove it, he turned around and asked me if I had a business card. Well, I did. And I gave it to him, whether he was serious about wanting it or not. He called me the next day, and we talked. We set our first date for March 1st, as we were only a couple of days away from the end of February. Of course the very next day was the big earthquake in Seattle, and we both took it as a sign. We were about to shake things up.

In March, my roommate announced to me that he was moving out, and I spent two months trying to find a new roommate. But by May, I had had no success, and I couldn't afford to spend another month in that apartment. My partner had asked me to move in with him, but I resisted because we didn't know each other that well. However, since I could not find another roommate, I took it as a sign from God that this was my next step, and I moved in with him.

One early morning in September, I was wakened about six a.m. by my sister. She told me to turn on my T.V. and watch. I'm so glad she called, since she was an employee of American Airlines. I turned on the T.V. and watched as a second plane hit the second World Trade Center Tower. Shortly after that they broke with the story of a third plane hitting the pentagon, and then another plane crashing in a field in Pennsylvania. I was overwhelmed. I just sat there. I felt as if we were at war and life as I knew it had ceased to exist. That's when we found out that two of the planes were American Airlines, and that they both originated in Boston. And that's when Rachel found out her best friend Jeff was on flight 11.

For many days after that Rachel would call crying because she was so distraught. She wondered if she had done enough to show him how much she appreciated what he had done for her. She wondered what he must have been thinking and experiencing those last few moments of his life. And she played over and over again a message that he left on her voice-mail the day before he left on that fateful flight. It was shortly after that that her husband had to take the phone off the hook because there was just too many people (other flight attendants) calling Rachel with more information on what had happened, and Rachel was overwhelmed. Jeff wasn't the only one she knew on the flight either. She had worked with just about every flight attendant on both of those planes.

It was only a few days later that I happened to be channel surfing, and I caught a conversation between Jerry Falwell and Pat Robertson, and they were talking about the terrorist attack. I was curious as to what they might say so I watched. Then I heard Jerry Falwell say, and I quote—"I blame the homosexuals for this."

My mouth dropped and I literally stood up in front of the T.V.

"Homosexuals?" I shouted back at the T.V. "Homosexuals? What the hell did we ever do to you? Every one of those terrorists was heterosexual. They were narrow-minded, fundamentalist, woman-hating, homo-hating freedom-suppressing, arrogant, abusive, hateful, religious zealots unable to cope with differing opinions— just like you! No religion in the history of the universe has a bloodier history than Christianity."

It was something like that. Unfortunately though, he wasn't able to hear it, and all I succeeded in doing was freaking out my neighbors upstairs. I couldn't understand why in the world he would blame us? Somehow in his mind we have come to represent everything that is evil in the world. How did that happen? Why did that happen? What is it about homosexuality that he hates so vehemently? Maybe, as Shakespeare once said, "Methinks he doth protest too much." I don't know. But I do know that I had nothing to do with September 11. In fact, I found it as horrible and disturbing as the rest of the country. If anything, the mentality of these hijackers more closely represented his views than they did mine. And as far as blame goes, it's been my experience that if you have to place blame for something then that means three things. One, you're unable to deal with the sin in your own life—two, you're unwilling to look at your own role in an event—and three, you're very judgmental.

THE AFTERMATH

It's been several years since that event, and I've never heard from Mickey or any of the rest of Exodus again. Eastside has never once contacted me. Despite all the work I did for them in my thirteen years there. It's sad, but there's a very wide gap between Christians and anyone who doesn't wear the cookie-cutter outfit. I slipped into that gap, and they didn't miss me.

This is where Christianity takes its stand. Now that I'm no longer in the mainstream, I've become their outcast. Were I willing to "repent," they would be there offering me platitudes and quotes from the Bible, but that's pretty much all I would ever get. Now that I was "In the Deathstyle" as Mickey called it, I've lost contact with people that I thought truly loved me.

On one hand I understand this. What's happened to me since I let go of my beach ball is challenging to the Christian on so many levels. Number one, they would have to deal with their own fears around the subject. Let's face it, homosexuality would not be such a huge issue if there wasn't so much fear and hatred mixed in. And, they don't want to have to leave the comfort of their beliefs.

I learned something along the way. Number one, we seem to define ourselves by our beliefs. I hear people say "I'm a Christian," "I'm an atheist," "I'm a Native American," "I'm an alcoholic," "I'm gay." Whatever it is, we place labels on ourselves and those labels are tags or definitions of who we think we are. We introduce ourselves based on those labels. Those beliefs take up residence in our psyche, and changing those beliefs requires us to find a new definition of ourselves. This is uncomfortable sometimes, and downright painful others.

There's one belief that goes deeper than any other. It seems to hang out very close to our Soul. That belief is our belief in God. This belief has greater power than any other belief we adhere to, and to take away this belief (or alter it) is to literally alter the very core of our being, and physically change who we are (yes, I do mean physically). I think that is why there's so much violence associated with the name of God. When you're that afraid, you have to change the world around you so that it doesn't threaten you at your deepest levels.

But that's the point. If God is to be understood and loved, then it must be at the level of our Soul. And I think that the one thing that made this transition possible for me was that I had learned to trust God early on, and I had learned to trust my relationship with God. I trusted God that he would let me discover myself, and that he would allow me to challenge my beliefs so that I could find that place where he and I could meet without so much clutter. It's what Christianity means when it talks about approaching God with a clean heart. It's what is meant when the Bible talks about stripping ourselves of false images, and it's what Jesus meant when he said that to find God you must first lose yourself. This isn't some platitude; this is God at Its most fundamental. And this was part of my process.

The fifteen years I spent trying to be straight were simply fifteen years trying to defend my idol, or my image of what God should look like based on certain facets that religion had created (and that I had bought in to). But in the process, I met God. The God I met dwells beyond time and space, dwells beyond the confines of the human heart, dwells beyond the big bang, and beyond evolution. I met this God (though a very small part of him to be sure) in my process of trying to accept what was happening to me as a gay man in a world that didn't allow homosexuality and spirituality to coexist.

Away from God and Back Again...
My Spiritual Journey

One thing that Eastside always encouraged me to do was to think for myself. The pastor of our church was a firm believer that we as his parishioners know what we believe based on our own research, not just what he told us, and I took him to heart. But it didn't really start there. If you'll recall, when I was living in Riverton I wanted to be a prophet, which meant, I wanted to know God from my own experience.

As I said earlier, I don't know where it came from, or what caused it to flourish, but I have always had a heart for God. I think about the scripture that reads "For the eyes of the Lord range throughout the earth to strengthen those whose hearts are fully committed to him..." 2 Chronicles 16:9. At an early age I made that connection with God, and for whatever reason, it took.

I also found that I loved theology and Bible study. At one point I was going to study it in college. Since finances prevented that, I decided to study it on my own. I studied Jewish culture and theology, I studied the history of Christianity, and I really got excited over the theology and philosophy of Christianity. But all that knowledge led to an interesting dichotomy. As time went on I began to understand how tenuous all this religion stuff was. I learned about the battles between the early church fathers over acceptable doctrine. I studied Christology and the battle over who Jesus really was in relationship to God. I read about the disputes between the Jewish disciples of Jesus family (led by James the brother of Jesus) and over the Gentiles (led by Paul) over who spoke for Jesus, and on and on and on.

All these things set me up for a "Faithquake." Suddenly I couldn't quote the Apostle's Creed with as much conviction as I once could. Many of the very foundations I once built my beliefs on were ripped away.

My journey away from God started with my first book, "The Warrior," which was published in 1995 (I came out—or was outed—in 2000). I was so excited. At last God was answering my prayers and I was going to be a published author. I signed the contract with the publisher in 1992. But as the years went on, and the book never seemed to make it into production for one reason or another, I was becoming more and more frustrated and despondent.

At long last the book was finally published and I started going out and doing the things that authors do. I scheduled book signings, talks, and other events to celebrate the book. But I would show up at the book signing only to learn that the bookstore couldn't get the book. Slowly things began to unravel. I then learned that the publisher had been raided by state of Utah and was brought up on some very serious charges. Not the least of which was embezzlement. I learned that they had embezzled thousands of dollars from me, and I wasn't ever going to see it again since they declared bankruptcy to avoid having to pay all this money back. On top of that, they owned the rights to my book.

I contacted an attorney who was recommended to me by a friend. She helped people in situations like mine, and she took on the case. She fought hard and got my rights back for me. In the end, she only charged me fifty dollars. The rights were mine, but the book wasn't. They had printed up several thousand, and as a result of the bankruptcy, their attorneys worked it out that I had no claim to them.

They set it up so that the authors would literally have to bid on their own books. But before anyone had that chance, an entrepreneur in Utah outbid everyone there. He was able to do so because he could buy all the books at once, and the courts felt that this was better. So every author with this company lost their books. I shouldn't say "lost." This man bought the books for about fifty cents a piece, and then tried to sell them back to the authors for much more. In my case, he tried to sell my books back to me at three dollars. I had just had several thousand dollars embezzled from me, and this guy went in and snatched my books away from me, and now he was asking me to buy them from him. When I told him that I was unable to afford the books, his response was that I would make it back when I sold them. I reminded him that selling books wasn't going to be that easy with no distribution, no marketing and no support behind me. So the books were gone.

How could I be so challenged over this? I was challenged because writing was my dream (one big one anyway). After so many years, it seemed as if God was finally allowing me an opportunity to fulfill my dreams, only to let them all fall apart. Did God look into my future and determine that I just wasn't ready? I couldn't get the nagging feeling out of my mind that I was never going to overcome my sexuality issues, and therefore God was never going to allow me to live out my dreams. Instead, he was going to dangle them over me like a carrot while I spent my whole life in complete futility. I was crushed. It was at this point that I began to consider that maybe it wasn't worth trying to overcome my sexuality after all, and in fact, I was ready to give up on God altogether. So to cope with these feelings, I took my grandfather's wedding ring and put it on my wedding finger. I considered this a difficult time in my relationship with God, but it was a relationship I planned to have forever, and the ring would act as a reminder that I was still in this relationship.

Oddly enough, I wasn't the only one suddenly hurled into the throws of this Godforsaken barren Neverland. A very close friend of mine, Jordan, was having his own issues with God. God had allowed something really horrible to happen to someone that was really close to him. His girlfriend had been raped at a party, and as a result, she ended up with some rather serious heath problems. For many days we would meet together and cry and pray and beg God to help us understand why our lives were in such disarray.

My other friend Bobby was having problems of his own. He was suffering some severe health issues in which he was nearly bedridden most of the time. As a result, he started looking into the issues and philosophies of Christianity to find out why all those things that he had put his faith and trust in, such as healing, weren't working.

So there were three of us, all struggling with serious God issues. In Bobby's case it was his health. In Jordan's case it was his girlfriend. In my case, it was my dreams (wrapped up in my sexuality). All of us were besieged over what to do with ourselves, with each other, and with God. During this bizarre period of my life, I had to literally rethink God, and what I was going to do as a Christian.

Another thing that kept running through my head was that night back at Eastside, with Kyle Martin and our prayer. Since the day it happened, I couldn't get what he said out of my head. But despite years of therapy and focus on prayer, and life with Exodus, nothing was changing. In fact, things were getting worse.

I stopped referring to God as God. I started referring to Him/It as "The Universe," or "Cosmic Intelligence" (if there was such a thing out there in the universe). But ultimately, deep down inside, I felt that if God did exist, He didn't give a shit about me, and so I wasn't going to give a shit about him either. But I never took off the wedding ring. Because I also hoped that I was wrong, and that God did give a shit about me, and that one day he would at least make an attempt to show me so. That's how I handled this crisis.

Bobby, on the other hand took the scientific approach. He studied science, physics, philosophy, and decided that atheism was the best solution for his problem. In fact, the universe was far too random, and God was "the opiate for the masses." Jordan, on the other hand, figured that maybe God didn't have as much control over the universe as we were taught as Christians and that maybe our purpose in life was to simply cope.

So there we were, the three of us falling apart and suffering from the total collapse of our spiritual infrastructure resulting from this so-called Faithquake. Jordan heard about a therapist who practiced a powerful form of therapy in Florida, and before we knew it, we were on a plane for Daytona Beach. What's a little more therapy in the scope of all that I had been through so far? And besides, who could pass up a trip to Daytona Beach Florida?

But afterwards, neither Jordan nor I felt that it had done us any good, and so we returned to Seattle to live with our crisis. We each handled our Faithquake differently, but we did try to rebuild. Eventually Bobby stopped worrying about science and decided that God was God and the Bible was truth, not science. Jordan started a Web site where he took on the issues between science and God, and he became an expert on many of the issues that center on this debate.

Me? Well, you just read my story. I managed to hang in there for a while, but things were changing radically. After this Faithquake I rebuilt too, but the foundation had shifted. I paid close attention to the conversations I had with Bobby and Jordan regarding the challenges we all had while trying reconcile God, science, the real world and our own lives.

The Moral of the Story

I used to say often that "Since I gave up on God I feel a lot better about him." I didn't think I was ready to face this "Dark Side of God." This is what I would call an ironic statement. At first, as I was walking through this, I had no idea that what was happening was actually healthy. I was a two-year-old/teenager learning to assert his independence. In the process of giving up on God, I learned how to think for myself, and to stop relying on someone or something for everything that I wanted my life to be. I learned that I was the driver of my life, not the passenger, and God was the car. God was the vehicle through which my life was lived, but I was the life and body, and it was up to me to move the car to wherever my chosen destination would be.

As I said earlier, our beliefs about God are about as close to the Soul as we can ever get. Therefore, whatever we believe about ourselves we believe about God at a deep level and whatever we believe about God we believe about ourselves. My journey away from Christianity was not a journey away from God though it looked that way at first. What it did was challenge me to look deeper into my soul, and give up my definition of God. In spiritual terms, I believe that's what it means to "die to ourselves," or to "take up our cross."

That led me to a renewed understanding of God. For the first time in my life I was no longer codependent on him. I could think for myself. This broke down the polarization I had build up in my mind regarding right and wrong. Things were no longer black and white, right or wrong, good or evil, but life now took up all shades of the gray scale. Black and white, right and wrong, good and evil all morphed into something that seemed to resemble different facets of a greater whole. I was now ready to meet God. And this time God was that force that animated me, that life that ran through me, and that element deep within my Soul that 'was my Soul.'

Many of my Christian friends believe that I have been duped by the Devil. They continue to ask me why I gave up on Jesus and turned my back on God. My first response to this question is simple. That's like asking a fish why it turned its back on the water. A fish can't live outside of the water. The water is everywhere, and the fish isn't even aware of it. No matter where that fish goes, it will always be in the water. It breathes in the water, it eats in the water, it drinks the water, and it even defecates in the water. Or you might ask me why I gave up on air? But air is everywhere. I live in it. It surrounds me. I take it into my being, it animates me, it cleanses the toxins from my body, and it gives life to every cell in my body. A fish out of water would die, and so would I if I were to stop breathing.

The same is true with God. No matter where I go, God is there. No matter what I do, God is there, and without him I would die. God is the universe. As C.S. Lewis once said in his classic book, "Parelandra:"

He dwells (all of Him dwells) within the seed of the smallest flower and is not cramped: Deep Heaven is inside Him who is inside the seed and does not distend Him. Blessed be He! Blessed be He!

And then again, he says this:

Where Maleldil [Maleldil is the name for God in this particular novel] is, there is the center. He is in every place. Not some of Him in one place and some in another, but in each place the whole Maleldil, even in the smallness beyond thought. There is no way out of the center save into the Bent Will which casts itself into the nowhere! Blessed be He!

Some people tell me that "I'm spiritually dead." I don't believe that's possible. The soul is eternal, and cannot die. Therefore there is no way that I could be dead. I believe that it's possible to poison the soul in its human incarnation, but you cannot kill it. Therefore, spiritually I am alive.

Since I gave up on God, I learned that I am a co-creator with God when it comes to my life. God has laid out a banquet table, which is the universe and all the choices that go with it, and I am free to make my choices, and those choices are based on what's right for me, not on some dogma or doctrine.

And the truth be told, I felt supported by God as I went through this whole process. While some of my friends thought that the outing by the police was "my sin being proclaimed from the rooftops," I really saw it as something else. For the few months before the event I was living a double life. I lived one life at church and one with those who were comfortable with their sexuality. I lived one life for my roommates, one life for Mickey, one life for my family and friends, and one life for myself. I was holding my beach ball under the water and it would not be suppressed.

What happened was God saying to me, "It's time for you to go out and live the life you were meant to live, and be the person you are." The event with the cops was just a little shove in that direction. The fact that I had a place to move to was an automatic answer to my dilemma. The second was that as soon as I moved to Capitol Hill, I found the job of a lifetime writing web content. It combined just about everything I wanted to do into one job. And I got that job mostly because of my address (they knew that a lot of gay men lived up on Capitol Hill, and it was an opportunity to hire a minority). The man that hired me was intrigued about where I lived and he felt that it was those qualities that would allow me to do the job better than any of the other candidates he had yet interviewed.

Natural disasters do happen, and when they do, people rebuild. But this time the house was bigger, and the foundation was stronger. Earthquakes, tornados, hurricanes, they all happen, and when they're over, we can see what was able to take the storm and what wasn't. Some disasters you can see coming, such as hurricanes, and sometimes tornados, and others you don't see, such as an earthquake, or in my case, a Faithquake. What matters is that we emerge from them realizing that the universe is a bigger place than we were aware of up to that point, and we learn what it means to be both vulnerable and in control at the same time. Natural disasters bring balance, they show us who we are in the greater scheme of things, and they point out our foibles if we let them. This is the nature of God, and this is what I took out of my life. I guess you could say, "This is the moral of my story."

Now Down to Brass Tacks

I look back on this book, and it seemed to get longer than I had originally anticipated. Originally, I had only meant to give a few, brief, details of my life and leave it at that, but then all these other things came into play. There was this event that sparked that event, and that event that sparked something else, and the only way to explain it was to actually go into more detail. Well now instead of being done, I realize that there's still a little more I must address or this manuscript would be incomplete.

I don't want to get into the fray of arguments around this issue, especially in regards to homosexuality and the Bible, but I do have to address some. There are many people, who are already explaining the spiritual/Biblical issues of homosexuality, but I must tackle at least a couple head-on, or this document would seem unfinished.

It's one of the favorite mantras of the Christian and they like to say it in their best Jerry Falwell voice. "It's against nature" they say as they position themselves in their most pious and self-righteous stance.

Well let's look at that statement. It's against nature for us to wear clothes. It's against nature for us to use a toilet instead of doing what the animals do. Where do animals go to the bathroom? Wherever they have to, whenever they feel the urge. It's against nature to get into a machine made of tin and drive it down the road at 60 to 80 miles an hour. It's against nature to build buildings into the clouds. It's against nature to get into a 60 ton machine and hurl yourself through the air thirty-thousand feet off the ground, at 600 miles per. It's against nature to marry one person and live with that person for the rest of your life (know of any animals that do that?). It's against nature to watch HBO and eat Ho-Hos. It's against nature to go into a person and cut away a cancer cell with light, it's against nature to get pregnant using artificial methods when it's already been shown that you can't have children. All these things are things that we don't do naturally, so why is it okay to do them now? The very fact that we're human is beyond anything that nature could have imagined. We are the only creatures on earth to be given the ability to reason, to think, and to hold ourselves accountable for our actions. We are the only creatures who can manipulate our environment with such energy.

That's part of what makes us unique as humans, we have an ability to do things that maybe aren't in our nature, such as fly in airplanes and send men to the moon. If you look at the animal kingdom (as many Christians want to do in trying to prove that nature doesn't behave this way), you will also find that there are many animals that don't have families. Most animals mate, and then the male of the species disappears and the mother is left to fend for herself. In some species, the mother even disappears soon after the young are born or hatched. Some mothers eat their young, some animals prey on other animals.

Not every sheep is born white. Some white cats have black spots. Some black cats have white spots. Wolves have very distinctive patterns. Trees and plants have different patterns. That's natural. The fact that some people would be gay or lesbian is a testament to nature and her love for diversity. Nothing in nature looks one-hundred percent like its counterpart, even at its most basic structure, the DNA.

I've often wondered if maybe homosexuality wasn't nature's way of slowing down the population so that she could guarantee enough room for everybody. As the old Jewish saying goes, "God makes more people, but he doesn't make more land." And right now, with the population of the planet expanding exponentially, aside from a major disaster, this is how nature's going to have to slow the population. If she had to do it another way, it would be more drastic and more violent. I prefer this way. So in that sense, we may even be saving the planet.

I've already addressed the Adam and Eve controversy. "In the beginning God created Adam and Eve, not Adam and Steve." In Seattle, where I live, there's been what I call "the Fish Wars." It started out with the Jesus fish on the back of many cars. Then someone took this fish and added legs to it and inside the fish inserted the word "Darwin." Then someone got a Jesus fish and showed it eating the Darwin fish. Then I saw a Darwin fish humping the Jesus fish. My favorite though, was the fish that used the Jesus fish symbol, but inside it said, "And chips." Now Christians have the fish with the word "Truth" written inside eating the Darwin fish.

What amazes me most about this fish is the word "Truth." In our generation, as science has literally changed our world (and our view of the world), there is still one group of people that refuse to deal with the truth. Why is that? The one group of people that should care most about the truth (and says they care most about the truth) is the one group of people that will go to the greatest lengths to avoid it or to try to change it. But they continue to claim that they "have" the truth. What I've discovered is that when they speak of truth, they're really talking about dogma. They have decided that their "dogma" is this thing called truth.

I don't argue it much anymore because it isn't worth it. No matter how the evidence piles up, there's a group of people that are determined to disprove and refute that evidence. If discrediting this evidence could be done, I would say "Great." It would be easier for me if I could just point to Eden and say "That's my heritage," but that's not where we are now.

I actually had a conversation like this once. I was talking with a girl one day who was down on Capitol Hill trying to proselytize and convert some homos (they like to come to Capitol Hill), and we were discussing the Adam and Eve scenario. That's when I told her what I'm telling you, what I believe about the evolution of our planet.

"Okay," was her response, "then where did the ape come from?"

Knowing where she was going from my own fifteen years as a Christian, I decided to play along with her just for fun.

"And where did the primordial goo come from?" she continued.

So I talked to her briefly about the Big Bang (although now I hear they're calling it "The Primordial Singularity").

"And where did the big bang come from?" she asked.

And so I explained to her what I knew about the process of the compression of matter until it heated up and exploded and began to form our universe (which, in all honesty isn't much, and what I do know is thanks to Kenneth R. Miller).

"And where did that matter come from?" she continued to ask, now with a smug smile on her face. She thought she had me. In her mind something had to start the whole thing rolling.

But that's when I asked her—"And where did God come from?"

Her answer: "Well, he always was."

"But that doesn't make sense," I responded.

"But he's God," she said, wondering why I wasn't seeing this very easy and simple logic.

Then I said—"If it's easy to believe that God just was, and that he's always been, isn't it just as easy to believe that the universe just was, and always was? If something can't come from nothing, then even God could not have come from nothing."

Now she was angry. "You have to believe in God! Everything has to start from something. You said it yourself; the universe was created by a big bang. Something started it."

"Well then," I asked. "Isn't it possible that God was created by that same explosion? Perhaps they both arrived together."

The discussion was over. I was rebuked in the name of Jesus, and condemned to burn in hell for all eternity for not believing in a loving God who wants me to be with him for eternity.

In his book "How to Know God," Deepak Chopra talks about this very issue—God is beyond all time. God wasn't "in the beginning," God was "from the beginning": A small, but radically important difference. I realize that I'm not doing this book justice, but I'm just trying to make a point. When we look at God we are looking at something beyond all that is, yet exists within all that is. What that means is that our experience with God can only be personal. I cannot tell you how to experience God, and you cannot tell me. To do so requires that we hold onto the idea of Adam and Eve because of our fear that there is no world outside of the Garden of Eden.

Then of course there's the perceived "Wrath of God" on Homosexuality based on the Stories of Sodom and Gomorrah. Most Christians are fully aware of this story, and they quote it with glee. For the sake of those who aren't familiar with this oft-told tale, I'll briefly recap so you'll have the basics.

I guess the first thing I should do here is introduce you to the cast of characters. At the top in a starring role is God and His costar is Abraham. In this particular story we don't see much of either, but they played a key role in the fate of Sodom and Gomorrah. Then there's Abraham's nephew, Lot, one of the residents of Sodom. Lot had a wife, and two daughters (both virgins as you will soon find out). And rounding off the cast are two angels. The setting takes place in the plains just north of the Dead Sea surrounded by cliffs and rocks.

In this infamous story God decided that he had had about as much as he could take from "The Cities of the Plain," which Sodom and Gomorrah were the two most famous. 'The stench of their sins" had reached him all the way into heaven is what he told Abraham one day during a visit. (That must have been some stench, since it would take thousand of years traveling at the speed of light just to get out of our galaxy let alone all the way to heaven.) Abraham pleaded with God not to destroy the cities if he found any righteous people living there, and God promised that he wouldn't as long as that provision was met.

Genesis 19 opens with two angels walking into Sodom (were they there to find the alleged "righteous" citizens, or were they there on reconnaissance?). Abraham's nephew, Lot, is sitting at the gate when he sees them. Based on the limited information of the story, we're assuming that the angles were there to check out the place, or to warn Lot, but that isn't made known. We don't even know what Lot was doing at the gate.

Lot sees the two angels and takes them to his house fearing their safety. But they don't get there unseen. That night all the men of the city show up to Lot's house demanding the two angels so that they may "know" (i.e. have sex with) them. Lot is appalled by their actions, so in order to save them, he offers in their place his two daughters who had "never known a man" (or had never had sex with a man). In other words, they were virgins. (I've got say, in that culture being a virgin wasn't necessarily a good thing.)

This act only made the men angrier and they threatened Lot with the same treatment. Just as the men reach Lot's front door, one of the angels pulls Lot back inside, and the men of Sodom are struck with blindness. They then tell Lot to take his family and get out of town that night before God rained down fire on them. He and his family were also warned not to look back.

Lot was rather attached to Sodom, so the angels literally took him by the hand and led him out of the city, telling him and his family to head for the hills. Lot protested and asked if he could head to a small nearby city. "It's a small city" he told the angels, so they agreed but he had to hurry. So for Lot's sake, they spared the city of Zoar.

Lot took his wife and his two daughters and they left Sodom just before dawn. As the angels promised, as Lot's family left the city, fire came down from Heaven. Lot's wife looked back and turned into a pillar of salt, thus proving throughout history, that God hates homosexuals and the women who look back upon them (i.e. fag-hags). But it turns out that Lot was still afraid and left Zoar and headed for the hills anyway, where he dwelt in a cave with his daughters.

What amazes me most about this story is that nobody seems bothered that God, of his own volition, would take it upon himself to come down to a city for the sole purpose of destroying men women and children. Isn't that out of character for a God of love? Is that how a loving father behaves toward any of his children? And what about these "men of Sodom?" Even in San Francisco, where huge amounts of men are gay, you would still be hard-pressed finding a situation where "every man in the city" would come out and demand to know two strangers (unless they looked like Brad Pitt or Orlando Bloom).

There are several other troubling events that nobody seems to care to discuss either. In my mind the most troubling thought is this—Lot is apparently considered a righteous man—even though he was willing to give up his two daughters to be raped by a mob of angry men to protect two people he didn't even know. The men of Sodom were considered evil because they wanted to have sex with two angels (adults), but were unwilling to rape two innocent girls (probably very young, eleven or twelve since they hadn't been with a man which usually happened at the age of thirteen or fourteen). Does that sound backwards? Granted, rape of any kind is unwelcome, but let's ask, "What kind of father would throw his own daughters to a mob of men like that, specifically emphasizing their virginity?"

Now Lot is a widower with the two daughters he was so ready to sacrifice only a few hours ago. While living in their cave, the two daughters decide that they don't want to die virgins, so they conspire to have children with the only man they know. They get their father drunk and then the oldest daughter sleeps with him. The next night they get their father drunk again, and the youngest daughter sleeps with him. Both girls get pregnant, and according to Genesis 19, their father had no recollection of what happened, and it happened twice.

This brings up some interesting questions which I won't address here, but that's a lot of alcohol. I've been pretty drunk before, but I'm pretty sure I would know if I committed incest (which wasn't officially banned until later in the book of Leviticus.) Lot's oldest daughter gave birth to a son and named him Moab. The youngest daughter gave birth to a son and named him Benammi a.k.a. Ammon. And if you know anything about the history of Israel, these two groups of people made things very difficult for the Tribes of Israel throughout most of their developmental years.

I must say, the God in this story doesn't sound like the father in the parable of the Prodigal Son. Nor does he seem to have a problem with a man that would offer up his two daughters to be raped by a mob of horny (and now angry) men. And what fully amazes me is that it seems that it's homosexuality, not incest that God finds repugnant. Genesis 19 strikes me not as much as a condemnation against homosexuality, but a stark reminder that God's family is far more dysfunctional than any of those who oppose it. Yet these are the family values that Jerry Falwell, Pat Robertson, Focus on the Family, and all the other far-right teachers keep trying to aver.

If you look at the reasons given for this horrific event, there aren't any. God tells Abraham that the stench of their sins has reached him but what was that stench? Did it smell like homosexuality? We're not told. But throughout the Bible, Sodom and Gomorrah have been chosen to represent sins other than sexual alternatives. Usually when you hear them mentioned, Sodom and Gomorrah are synonymous with greed and selfishness not with homosexuality. The only reference to the sins of Sodom and Gomorrah is in Ezekiel 16, where God accuses them of being greedy and selfish. He also claims that they didn't help the poor and needy, the widow and the orphan. And then He (God) accuses Israel of being worse than Sodom and Gomorrah.

Another thing that frightens Christians is the perceived attack on "Family Values," specifically, "Biblical Family Values" that homosexuality represents. I remember receiving an e-mail at work from a friend. It seemed a certain domestic brewery was planning to use a homosexual couple in one of their beer advertisements. In my friend's "concern," she sent around e-mail to everyone on her e-mail list asking them to write to the company and protest the advertisement and to threaten to ban the company all together. Of course at the time I was still hiding out in the closet so she sent it to me thinking that I felt the same way she did. So in jest, I sent back an e-mail asking her if she knew the number to support the ad. She responded by sending back another e-mail reminding me, "I couldn't be serious," among other things, and that got me upset. So I sent back another e-mail to this effect.

First of all, I asked, are Christians really supposed to be frequenting establishments like this? Her response to that was that she had a problem with the ad. She didn't want her children, and her nieces and nephews growing up under the influence of "this abomination." Now I was really upset. Friend or not, I was not going to be silent about that.

What I've noticed about Christianity in general, is that they're looking for some kind of utopia. Some place where they can live in peace and harmony. Some place where everyone thinks and acts as they do. Some place where there's no freedom of choice, no freedom of expression. Everybody's doing the same thing all the time, and nobody's offending them. It sounds like a nice world, but it isn't the world that I live in. And the last time we tried to create it, we had a little thing called the Salem Witch Trials.

I remember watching the news one day, just after the Monica Lewinsky story broke. They were interviewing protesters, and I saw one self-righteous man reach into his wallet and pull out a picture of his kids and show it to the reporter. "What am I going to tell my kids?" he asked. My thought at the time was, "Tell them the truth" as carefully as you can to a child, and then help them understand how much trouble the president is in, and why." To me, this was the perfect opportunity to teach the children about actions and consequences.

As a gay man, it's frustrating being responsible for everybody else's kids. They don't want me being gay because they don't want their kids growing up in an environment where gay people are given voice. They don't want me speaking my mind because their kids might hear me and soften their views toward me, and that would bring them mental distress, and challenge their perfect utopian beliefs.

I agree that children are impressionable and that they should be offered as much protection as we can healthily give them, but to shelter them from the world around them does them a great disservice, since sooner or later they're going to have to grow up and live in this big bad world. And any person bringing children into the world does so at their own risk and shouldn't expect society to change the rules because of their choice to have a child.

They're using homosexuals in beer commercials (which I think is odd, because most of us drink white wine spritzers or martinis). I think that if you want to make the world a better place, teach the children about the world—it's got its ups and its downs, and there are a whole plethora of people living in it. I wonder if we try and shelter children from the world, they may become like us: unable to deal with diversity, and striving desperately to make everyone else around them conform rather than learning how to live with their neighbors. Isn't this what causes wars? Six billion people are a lot of people to try and change, but one person, the person you see when you look into the mirror every morning, that's much easier.

And let's talk about this whole Biblical Family Values issue. Let's look at the greatest men of the Bible, and their families, starting with Adam and Eve, and their sons Cain and Abel. It's a fairly common story, but again, for those of you unfamiliar with it, here's the basic storyline from Genesis 4.

Cain, the older brother was a farmer, or as the Bible says "tilled the soil," and Abel, the younger brother was a shepherd. He "kept the flocks." Both of them appeared before God to offer up a sacrifice. "Cain brought some of the fruits of the soil as an offering to the Lord." And Abel brought "fat portions from some of the firstborn of his livestock." The Lord looked favorably on Abel's offering but for some reason he didn't look so favorably on Cain's. We aren't ever told why, but it made Cain somewhat jealous. There is a conversation where God tells Cain that if he will do what is right, then God will look favorably on his sacrifice, but again, we're never told specifically what it is God is looking for (isn't that always the way with parents).

So Cain set up a meeting with his brother somewhere in the field, and when they were there, "Cain attacked his brother Abel and killed him."

Then God asked Cain, "Where is your brother Abel?"

Cain replied "I don't know. Am I my brother's keeper?"

God knew where Abel was and of course he was angry with Cain, and cursed him so that when he worked the ground it would no longer yield its crops to him. He also told Cain he would be a restless wanderer on the earth. So the first thing Cain did was get a wife of his own (presumably one of his sisters), and have kids and build a city in the land of Nod (I guess he could have been restless: what with traffic and the noisy neighbors upstairs, and those damn kids and their music blaring at 120 decibels).

The great patriarch and founder of Israel, Abraham, always wanted a son. God, on many occasions promised Abraham that his children would be like the 'sands of the sea,' or like 'the stars in the sky.' But by eighty-six Abraham was still childless. So Abraham's wife Sarah had a wild idea. She had an Egyptian servant named Hagar, and she told Abraham to take Hagar as his wife and marry her.

As luck would have it, Hagar "conceived" as the Bible puts it. But things didn't go well between her and Sarah. Apparently she "began to despise her mistress." So Sarah goes to Abraham once again, and while this whole affair was her idea, she blamed Abraham.

"You are responsible for the wrong I am suffering" she told Abraham.

Abraham responded by saying "Your servant is in your hands. Do with her whatever you think best."

So Sarah mistreated Hagar, and Hagar fled. The Angel of the Lord found Hagar near a spring in the desert and told her to go back and submit to her mistress. So Hagar returned and bore Abraham's first son, Ishmael. However, it was Isaac, Abraham's second son from Sarah that got all of the press, and Abraham's blessings; not Ishmael.

We like to think of Jacob, younger twin of Esau, son of Isaac and grandson of Abraham as one of the great patriarchs of the Bible. But Jacob was a cheat, a liar, and a thief. First he used extortion to get his brother's birthright. His brother Esau, who was a hunter, came to him hungry. Jacob would only feed him in return for Esau's birthright as the older brother.

Then when it came time for Isaac to give his sons the final blessing before he died (which included the inheritance of all his possessions), his mother concocted a scheme. "When Isaac was old and his eyes were so weak that he could no longer see, he called for Esau his older son." Sensing that Isaac was about to give Esau the blessing, Rebekah, Jacob's mom, dressed her younger son to look and smell and feel like Esau. Thus Jacob again got the blessing that was supposed to go to Esau.

But his deception doesn't end there. The list of Jacob's deceptions covers several chapters of the book of Genesis.

Aaron, the brother of Moses, also the first high priest of Israel in the Sinai desert, had two sons, Nadab and Abihu. They also were ordained as priests by God and by Moses. Then for some reason they decided to disrespect the temple and "they took their censers, put fire in them and added incense, and they offered unauthorized fire before the Lord, contrary to his command."

If there's one thing you'll learn quickly as you read through the Bible, "Don't piss God off." Well Nadab and Abihu did just that. So fire came from the presence of the Lord and consumed them. And Aaron was told that he wasn't to morn his two sons.

In the book of Judges, there's another fine example of Biblical Family Values. In Judges 11, a man named Jephthah was locked in a battle with the Ammonites. In hopes to win the battle against the Ammonites, Jephthah promised God that "If you give the Ammonites into my hands, whatever comes out of the door of my house to meet me when I return in triumph from the Ammonites will be the Lord's and I will sacrifice it as a burnt offering." Well shucks, wouldn't you know it, the first person out the door was his daughter and only child, dancing to the sound of tambourines.

When Jephthah saw his daughter, he tore his clothes and told her of his vow to the Lord. All in all she was very understanding. "My father," she replied. "You have given your word to the Lord. Do to me just as you promised." But then she makes one more request. Kind of an odd request, but it makes sense. "Give me two months to roam the hills and weep with my friends, because I will never marry."

So she went away and wept over her virginity for two months, and then returned. Personally, I would have gotten the hell out of there, but she didn't. Instead she returned home and her father "did to her as he vowed."

The stories of David and his family are great family stories.

David sleeps with Bathsheba while her husband is away at war. Soon she reveals to him that she's pregnant, so David has her husband, Uriah the Hittite return home from battle in the hope that he will sleep with his wife and David will be off the hook. But Uriah is loyal to his king (David), and he does not sleep with his wife. Instead, he sleeps at the entrance of the palace with all David's servants. So David tries another approach. This time he sends Uriah to the battle front with a letter to his general, Joab. Uriah isn't privy to the information in this letter (although he delivered it), or he may have been more reluctant to pass it on. In this letter David told Joab to put Uriah on the front lines of battle, and as soon as it got heated, Joab and his men were to pull back, and Uriah would be left alone. And that's exactly what happened. Uriah was dead, and now David was free of a scandal.

Later in the story, David's son Amnon falls in love with his sister Tamar. "He became frustrated to the point of illness" because it was impossible for him to do anything to her. So he set up a little scheme. He had his friend Jonadab tell Tamar that Amnon was ill so that she should minister to him. It worked. Amnon pretended to be sick and David sent Tamar to take care of him. When she arrived, Amnon raped her, but once he had his jollies, "he hated her." "He hated her with intense hatred. In fact, he hated her more than he had loved her."

He told her to get out.

She told him that making her leave would be an even greater crime than the rape itself, but they threw her out and bolted the door behind her. She could no longer wear the robes of a virgin because of her attack and she could no longer marry either because of the customs in Israel.

Tamar was Absalom's favorite sister. He loved her deeply, and when he heard this he became very angry, setting the scene for his attempted coup d'état several years later.

Absalom did have his revenge. He took his brother to a celebration at Baal Hazor. When his brother was in high spirits from excess wine, then Absalom's servants slew him as they were instructed by Absalom. And yet Absalom is portrayed as the bad guy.

Ironically, the one king who had a good child was Saul, the father of Jonathan—of David and Jonathan. Jonathan was true to David, true to God and true to Israel, and yet God took away the kingdom from Jonathan and handed it over to David who wasn't really true to anyone but himself.

Go figure.

I would also like to point out that David never met a woman he didn't marry. Between him and his son Solomon, they probably married half the known female population back then. It was common back then for men to have many wives, and women were just property.

These are just some of the stories in the Bible. These are the family values Christians are afraid that homosexuality is somehow threatening. To be completely honest, I don't care how great the Bible says these men were; I do not share their family values. Christianity talks at great lengths about love, but this is not love. And Jesus didn't change that. He was very clear that he "came to turn mother against daughter and father against son." When approached by his own family he publicly disowned them claiming that only those who listened to him were his family.

The family values of the Bible do not constitute family, or even value. As I've read through these stories, the one thing I've noticed missing throughout all of them is just that—"values." These are highly dysfunctional people who should not be emulated, but should instead serve as a stark reminder of how important it is that we as humans develop spiritually so that we no longer propagate these kinds of behaviors.

What threatens Biblical Family Values is not homosexuality, not television, not rock and roll, not Democrats, not even pornography, or a president getting a hummer in the Oval Office. What threatens Biblical Family Values is the Bible itself. As we humans become more "civilized," these behaviors are no longer acceptable to us. We are learning that we should no longer tolerate violence of any form against children. We are learning that it is deplorable to tolerate the subjugation of women or the proliferation of slavery. We are learning that families must act responsibly toward one another and the communities around them if the human race has any chance at all. And even in the name of God we are learning to find these things appalling and unacceptable. These Biblical events may have been acceptable in a time where survival was much more difficult, but it is no longer acceptable, and that's why Biblical Family Values are under attack. What society as a whole is now looking for is a place where children are loved and cherished, a place where all children are taken care of, fed and nurtured, and we're less concerned about what that family has to look like.

I knew a lot of Christians growing up, and there's one thing I can tell you. Most of their upbringing wasn't good. If you look at the basic structure of most churches, you will see that they're set up to keep children down, to suppress women, and to control their members. This is where today's society is finally starting to break free. I believe that if every child on this planet were to know they were loved and cherished (not that homosexuality was wrong), then we would have heaven on earth.

I once saw a television talk show where they discussed gay adoptions. All throughout the show one man in particular kept protesting that if they allowed gay adoptions then the kids would turn out gay. My first thought to this argument was that every gay and lesbian person I had ever met was the product of "straight" parents, not gay parents. My parents were both straight. Sexuality is in the hard drive, not the software. I can't share my gay software with anyone, no matter how much I wish I could. And believe me; I had a lot of friends who would have been perfect candidates for my file-sharing software, were that possible.

I'd also like to use a little bit of math. For some reason people compare sexuality (hard drive) to environment (software). I can understand because it looks so similar. So this is where the math comes in. Let's say I have an equation. It looks something like this: $X^3 + X^2 + X$ and I'm told to simplify that down as far as I can go. Can I simplify this any further? The answer is no. While X^3 and X^2 and X may look similar, in fact they are three completely different integers. That is the best way I can think of to try and explain the differences between sexuality and environment and upbringing. They're very different.

Another thing that bothered me about this man's arguments was that in his obsession with averting any more homosexuality in the world he lost sight of something that I think is even more important. Most of those kids that are up for adoption are kids that don't or wouldn't have a family life without it. They're products of parents who didn't want them, or couldn't keep them, or they're in the foster care system or some other life tragedy. And despite the fact that there are people out there who would love to take these kids and give them a chance at life, this man would rather that these kids stay in their troubled lives rather than find the support of someone who loves them, just because he didn't care for the disparity from his own viewpoint. That to me is ultimately the biggest tragedy. It reveals that Christians are not Pro-Life. Life is about diversity, about love, and about making sure that all those in need are being supported and loved. They're just anti-abortion, and that's completely different. Don't abort the kid, but once they're born, they're on their own. And if they commit a crime, then we can kill them.

Then, of course there's the infamous four: The four verses in the Bible that ban homosexuality. Here they are in their entirety so that you can see them for yourself.

The first one shows up in a list of sexual prohibitions in the book of Leviticus.

"Do not lie with a man as one lies with a woman, that is detestable.

LEVITICUS 18:22

If a man lies with a man as one lies with a woman, both of them have done what is detestable. They must be put to death; their blood will be on their own heads.

LEVITICUS 20:13

Therefore God gave them over in the sinful desires of their hearts to sexual impurity for the degrading of their bodies with one another.

They exchanged the truth of God for a lie, and worshiped and served created things rather than the Creator—who is forever praised. Amen.

Because of this, God gave them over to shameful lusts. Even their women exchanged natural relations for unnatural ones.

In the same way the men also abandoned natural relations with women and were inflamed with lust for one another. Men committed indecent acts with other men, and received in themselves the due penalty for their perversion.

ROMANS 1:24-27.

> Do you not know that the wicked will not inherit the kingdom of God? Do not be deceived: Neither the sexually immoral nor idolaters nor adulterers nor male prostitutes nor homosexual offenders...
>
> 1 Corinthians 6:9

> And that is what some of you were.
>
> 1 Corinthians 6:11

Well there you have it. That seems pretty cut and dry. You can't argue with those injunctions can you? But let's look at what else Paul said in Corinthians, just a few verses later.

> Now for the matters you wrote about. It is good for a man not to marry. But since there is so much immorality, each man should have his own wife and each woman her own husband.
>
> 1 Corinthians 1:1-2

Christians love to use this verse as a ban on Gay marriages, saying that true marriage is a union of one man, and one woman, but Paul is really just making concessions to those who can't handle their morality.

> I say this as a concession, not as a command.
>
> 1 Corinthians 7:6

> But if they cannot control themselves, they should marry, for it is better to marry than to burn with passion.
>
> 1 Corinthians 7:9

Paul also has some other commands right alongside the ban on homosexuality, and I don't see these rules enforced anymore.

> Every man who prays or prophesies with his head covered dishonors his head. And every woman who prays or prophesies with her head uncovered dishonors the head—it

is just as though her head were shaved. If a woman does not cover her head, she should have her hair cut off, and if it is a disgrace for a woman to have her hair cut or shaved off, she should cover her head.

1 CORINTHIANS 11:4-6

Judge for yourselves: Is it proper for a woman to pray to God with her head uncovered? Does not the very nature of things teach you that if a man has long hair, it is a disgrace to him, but that if a woman has long hair, it is her glory? For long hair is given to her as a covering. If anyone wants to be contentious about this, we have no other practice—nor do the churches of God.

1 CORINTHIANS 11:15

In Leviticus, there's an injunction that says "Do not come near a woman during her period of uncleanness to uncover her nakedness." Leviticus 18:19. I don't hear that one preached from the pulpit too often. In Leviticus 20:18 the same injunction is repeated, just a little differently. "If a man lies with a woman in her infirmity and uncovers her nakedness, he has laid bare her flow and she has exposed her blood flow; both of them shall be cut off from among their people."

In Leviticus 20:8 it reads, "You shall faithfully observe My laws. I the Lord make you holy."

Let's look at that closely. According to this passage, God's laws are to be obeyed. But let's understand this. There isn't anything in this scripture that says "some of my laws." Jesus even went so far as to say if you break one commandment, you've broken them all. In the Pentateuch, there are over six hundred laws, and if we want to take one out of there, then we've got to take them all out. That means you can't show deference to the rich. You can't sow two types of seed in the same field. You can't eat blood if you eat meat. There are several types of meat you can't eat. There were many laws about sacrificial lambs and scapegoats, and holidays and religious ceremonies and cleanliness. You can't just lift one of the scriptures out of this passage unless you're prepared to use them all. This is true of Leviticus, and Corinthians.

In my copy of the Torah, translated from Hebrew by the Jewish Publication Society, they have this to say about this particular verse.

> Far more controversial, from the modern standpoint is the outright condemnation of sexual relations between males— conduct for which the death penalty is prescribed. We have no record of a death sentence for this crime being carried out under Jewish auspices....
>
> In his famous 1935 letter to the concerned mother of a homosexual man, Sigmund Freud wrote, "Homosexuality is assuredly no advantage, but it is nothing to be ashamed of, no vice, no degradation, it cannot be classified as an illness." ...
>
> In many cultures there has been little or no objection to homosexual behavior. The ancient Egyptians condemned it, but it was widespread among the Greeks. In the Athens of Pericles and Plato, love affairs between teenage boys and older men were frequent and were even considered beneficial for the intellectual and moral development of the younger party. Even in societies that officially ban such practices, they occur more frequently than former generations supposed— or at least admitted. Homosexual behavior has also been noted among lower animals as well...
>
> Our greatest needs at present are to gain more knowledge on the subject—knowledge which is sought objectively— and to insure that individual reactions to this admittedly sensitive subject do not result in the denial of simple justice and fairness of homosexual women and men.
>
> THE TORAH—A MODERN COMMENTARY pp881-883
> EDITED BY W. GUNTHER PLAUT
> PUBLISHED BY THE JEWISH PUBLICATION SOCIETY

But it can be argued that the command was reaffirmed in the New Testament, so that makes it credible, right?

When I talk about my experiences, someone will often approach me and say, "But I know someone who's changed." I even sometimes talk to those who tell me they have succeeded. But I know far more people who have abandoned any semblance of spirituality simply because they couldn't beat this thing, and God didn't seem at all interested in helping them. Because of the rhetoric in the church today, they don't believe that you can be spiritual and be gay at the same time.

But again, let's look at the hard drive. It has been noted that there is a spectrum of sexuality.

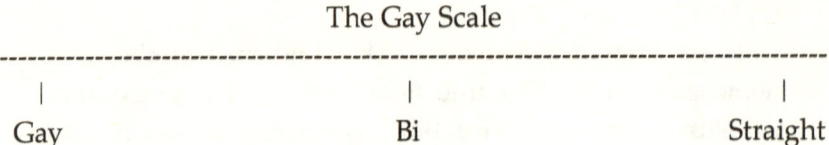

The Gay Scale

Gay   Bi   Straight

Depending on where you are on this line I think has a lot to do with how successful you're going to be at any attempt to change. Those in the middle of the Gay/Straight line can focus their attention to one side or the other, and they can live there comfortably for quite some time. They would be what we called bi-sexual.

Others find that they would like to experiment and see what it's like, but that's just because they're a little further away from "straight" on the scales. But there are also those of us who are definitely on the "gay" side of this spectrum. I've seen interviews with those who have claimed they have changed (there aren't very many, but there are a few) and they always seem to be closer on the scale toward straight. But I've also read many reports by those who thought they had changed and then all of a sudden they uprooted their families and tore their lives apart because they just couldn't "continue to live a lie." It's the beach ball syndrome all over again. Only this time, unfortunately, there were other people involved.

I read a book very early on in my life as a Christian called "Beyond Rejection," and the man who wrote it claimed that he was raped by his step father. As a result, he too found himself gay. But in reality, I don't think that's how it worked. What I hear most often about child abuse and molestation, is that the child perpetuates the abuse continually in their development as they grow and mature. That means if a child was raped by a same-sex parent or adult, then the child may perpetuate that abuse for many years, trying to deal with all the emotions that were present during the experience. In which case, as the abused adult seeks help and works through those issues, their true sexuality will be restored to them. Notice what I said here. Their true sexuality will be restored.

Just about every gay person I've ever talked to tells me the same thing. They all knew they were different by the age of ten and before. Like I said earlier, it's not a choice, it's a discovery. As I go through this explanation with people, they respond—"But Mickey did it. He's successful. He's a father with two teenage boys. He leads an Ex-Gay group and helps others overcome their sexuality. That means he's been successful for at least that long."

Mickey used to tell a story during our meetings about something that happened between him and his mom. When his mom found out that he was gay, she stood in the middle of the room and tore up his picture, and announced to him that Mickey was no longer her son. Mickey cried and said "I'll change mama, I promise."

Mickey's mom has been dead for some time, but based on what I've heard about his relationship with her, it was intricate. I think there's a lot more going on around that issue, and I don't know if Mickey has dealt with that or not. But by his own admission though, Mickey has said often that he has to avoid Seattle (especially the Capitol Hill Area) and he encourages others to do so. And before I left the Exodus group, Mickey was diagnosed with colon cancer. I remember at the time wondering if it had something to do with his decision to try and force a change that wasn't meant to be. Of course that's the more esoteric thinking in that sometimes the cancer has deeper issues. But that's between him and his body, and of course, God to work out, those were just questions I had when I heard the news (and thank God it was treated and the last I heard he was doing okay).

And there's the all-time classic, "It's the Mother/Father's fault." I once had a guy try and tell me that 'the reason I was gay was because of the relationship I had with my father.' Now I've had many people tell me that, and at one time that's what I believed, but what made this one stand out was my response to him. I started laughing. Then I asked him, "Do you know anyone... anyone at all... someone whose brother's sister's, father-in-law's son's college roommate's best friend's little brother's step-dad's daughter's friend... who has had a good relationship with their father?"

I was a Christian for nearly sixteen years, and in that time I have seen just as many bad Christian fathers as I have ever seen outside the church. And quite frankly, inside the church it's worse because the fathers can be abusive and the children have to take it because they're Biblically obliged to submit to their parents. Absalom and Solomon had a rotten father, but they weren't gay. Isaac's father tried to kill him, but he wasn't gay. Cain's father was God's first son, and Cain didn't turn out so well (at least according to legend).

Parenting plays a big role in the upbringing of a child but let's face it, most of us have had some difficult times with our parents. Even if our parents tried to be good parents, they're only human, which means that many mistakes were made. Even Jesus had issues with his parents. That's just the nature of growing up on planet earth. And there are certain issues that will get exaggerated and certain problems that can be created by certain styles of parenting, but that's like saying a bad parent can make you shorter, or taller, or a different sex all together.

LOOKING BACK

As I look back on what was originally only meant to be a small article I realize that I'm still not finished. There's so much more that I haven't even touched on.

I only want to restate what I said at the beginning. The God that I discovered throughout my struggle emerged in a way that I could have never expected or understood. This God looks so much different than the Christian God, but only because this God is now able to be itself without having to fit into my image of how it should look. This God is so much more powerful, and so much closer to my soul. This God really is about love, and this God really is about compassion for his children. (I know that I've used the masculine for God during this article, but that's because I relate to God more in the masculine sense than the feminine.) I've never denied that I was deprived of a decent father, and I've never denied that the breakdown in that relationship hasn't caused some problems, but I've learned over the years that even something that deep is really very shallow when it comes to the soul. Let me explain.

I like to use the metaphor of a child flying a kite. The child is small, and getting the kite into the wind is challenging. If the child's parent is there to help that child, then the kite goes into the air easier because the parent has the height and know-how to lift the kite. Without the parent, the child may have a harder time. Either way, the kite still goes into the air and still flies once the child figures out how to use the wind. To some that may seem rather simplistic as they believe that I'm not dealing with the core issues of parent child relationships. So let me just add one little change. We are that kite. Our parents are here to help us and guide us so that we may soar into the wind like the kite. Some of us didn't have the parental guidance we needed, and we found that we had to struggle harder to get our kites—our soul—into the air. But we did it. Once in the air, what happened on the ground is no longer relevant (provided we break the strings that tie us down and prevent us from soaring). That doesn't mean it didn't hurt. That doesn't detract from what happened. But even if you had the best parents in the world, you've still got to get off the ground. Your parents can only get you so far. Conversely, there's only so much they can do to hold you down too. The soul was meant to fly, and every soul wants to fly. So any soul that opens up even slightly finds itself discovering ways to hoist itself into the winds of change.

That's where forgiveness comes in. And when I use the term forgiveness, I'm not talking about forgive and forget, I'm talking about losing yourself in God, and allowing God to become those areas in your life where you feel that you have been damaged. For instance, in my case, my father took away from me my right to defend myself. He used to laugh when other kids would beat me up, but he would never allow me to fight back. I grew up thinking that I wasn't worth defending. In the forgiveness treatments that I did for my father, several things happened.

First of all, I acknowledged everything I believed my father did to me that caused me pain and grief. I didn't just acknowledge, I got in touch with the anger, and I wrote it all down on paper in big dark bold letters. I told him everything that he did and why I hated him.

Then for everything that I felt was taken from me by my father, I acknowledged that those very aspects were found in God. God became that parent that would support me, and would stand up for me, and would teach me how to defend myself. God became what I needed in a father, and he did it far more completely than my original father ever could.

Once I realized that God was those things that I felt I needed from my father, then I turned my need to judge this man over to God. While this wasn't exactly easy, it wasn't hard either. It was mostly just dealing with the ego and the ego wanted retribution for the sins that were committed against me.

I'm in the air now, though I don't know if I would say that I'm soaring. But I am aware that there's a great height that I can now attain, and I don't need that weight of unforgiveness holding me down. Just like in Peter Pan, 'In order to fly you have to think happy thoughts,' and the only way to get happy thoughts is to learn to forgive. That doesn't mean that the experiences of the past are meaningless, it just means that I gave them new meaning. Instead of accepting the label of victim, I turned this experience into something completely different. This experience means to me that I now have a mission. It's my turn to enter the fray. It's my turn to talk about what I've been through, and to help Christians understand why I could try to change for fifteen years, and then realize that it wasn't necessary. I want to talk to my fellow homosexuals, and tell them that they can be spiritual; find God; AND be gay. I want to talk to anyone who wants to understand this topic more and let them know that things aren't always what they seem. This is the new meaning I have put on my life and my experience. That's what forgiveness has allowed me to do.

I have one last thing to say, and that is I want to make perfectly clear that I am not anti-Christian. The reason so much of this article is directed at Christians is simply because Christians make the most noise about it. They're the ones who feel so strongly that they must squelch this issue. Were it not for Christianity, I don't think there would be a need to write this article. As I pointed out earlier, the Jewish religion is taking this all in stride, and they are actively debating it. Not to find ways to stop it, but to understand it. In my town there are several synagogues that allow gay people to come and worship without any fear of reprisal.

And as far as Muslims go, I know very little about their faith, but they're not lobbying congress and trying to rally their congregations together to censure this particular group of people. That's why this article may seem so pointed toward the Christian. But that's why it must be talked about. When a group of people believes that they have the only way to God, they become dangerous, and that's what I hope to prevent. There can be no One Way to God. God is infinite, and based on simple physics it would be impossible to limit those options.

That being said, I would like to leave with a little parable I wrote a while back. Jesus liked to tell stories, and I think stories are the best way to communicate. This story is in the form of a dream.

THE BLACK SHEEP

Last night I had a dream.

It was the strangest dream that I had ever had, and when I woke up I had to write it down.

In this dream I saw a birth. It was a baby lamb.

As the lamb came into the world, his parents, the Ewe and the Ram looked lovingly upon him, doting over him incessantly. In my dream they named him Lanny.

Lanny was such a precious little life, naked with nothing but its mother and father to care for him.

As Lanny grew he began to develop wool. That's when things started to go wrong for him.

The wool Lanny grew was black as night.

The little lamb looked at its reflection in the pond and noticed his wool was black and not white like his mother's and father's or his brother's and sister's in the flock.

As he stood there staring at his reflection he felt an overwhelming sense of fear creep over him, and in my dream I felt that terror wash over me too. What was he to do?

He searched around and found some cotton in a nearby field. He sauntered over to the field casually so that nobody would see him. Once there, he rolled in the cotton so that it covered every part of his skin so that nobody could see the black.

The thorns and sticks from the cotton cut into his skin, and he hurt terribly, but he was safe from the ridicule of the rest of the flock.

For a very long time this went on, he could cover himself with cotton and protect his identity.

Nobody noticed.

Then one day the sheerer came to visit the flock. One by one he rounded the sheep and sheered off their excess wool.

Lanny watched in horror and tried to hide. But it was no use. Just as he was sneaking away, he was noticed by the sheerer and brought forward. The sheerer took his sheers and clipped the wool away, revealing to the flock that the little lamb had actually been wearing cotton to cover up his black wool.

Lanny was found out. He was so ashamed. The rest of the flock stared at him in disbelief.

"How could this happen?" the Ram asked. "My family and I are upstanding members of this flock. I am a white sheep. I have white wool. My wife has white wool. All my other lambs have white wool."

Lanny only hung his head in shame. "I'm sorry father" he said. "I tried to cover it up." He looked at the rest of the flock. "I've done everything I could to be like you" he said, "but my wool keeps coming through black."

"Black wool is a choice" one of the ewes whispered in a snit. "All you have to do is choose to have white wool and you will."

"Black wool is a sign of a perversion" another ram shouted. "You're wearing black wool because you're sick. You're not right. You're a freak of nature"

"Maybe it's an abnormality?" another sheep questioned. "Perhaps if we took him and reprogrammed him he would grow white wool and be normal like us."

"All you need to do is make your hair white and you'll be fine" another sheep shouted.

And soon it was decided that this little lamb would be brought before the council. At the head of the counsel was an old ram that had been in the flock for many years. He was considered wise and well respected by the rest of the flock.

He looked the little lamb over very carefully.

"I've seen such a thing before" he said. "For some reason nature adds a little touch of spice to the poor creature and he stands out. Unfortunately she does not consider how the poor creature will suffer due to his difference."

He looked back at the crowd. "I suggest he's just fine. Give him room and let him be. Accept him as your son and your brother and fellow flock member."

The sheep bleated and turned their backs on the elder. They would do no such thing. This was a black sheep and he had no place in their society.

While they were discussing what to do with the poor little lamb, another ram who considered himself wise approached them.

"I have seen such things too" he said. "And unlike my foolish collogue I have a solution. I have a friend who has worked with lambs like yours, and he has found a solution until your lamb can repent and grow into his white wool."

So they sent the little lamb to this special flock. They called themselves the "Recovering White Wool" flock. In this flock were many other lambs and sheep like himself who had once had black wool. But now they had white wool. Their wool was so white in fact that Lanny wondered if they were really sheep at all.

The leader of the flock, Jefferson, got up and introduced Lanny to the rest of the group. Then he went on to explain—"Having black wool is not a choice, it's a discovery. But it is against nature and therefore we must change it. If we allow ourselves to continue with our black wool, will eventually be cut from the flock and not allowed access to the good shepherd."

As soon as he was done talking, Jefferson took Lanny and lay him down in the field. Then he mixed up a special dye. The dye stank and made Lanny's eyes water. When they put it on his wool, Lanny's skin started to burn and his nose swelled up. He could hardly breathe.

Jefferson looked him over. "Now go look at yourself in the pond" he said.

Lanny did and he was surprised at what he saw. His wool was white like bleach. There was no trace of the black. But his skin itched and burned for several days.

Soon he forgot that he was a black sheep, and took his place with his flock.

But sheering time came again, and his wool was once again sheered from his body.

When they took off his wool, his skin was exposed. It was course, and chapped. It cracked and bristled. His skin was so sensitive that even the air made it hurt.

As the hair began to grow back, it was like having thousands of little needles sticking into his skin.

The pain was so terrible that he went off by himself to be alone and cry.

Soon the skin had begun to heal somewhat and he could move without wincing.

Just as he was starting to feel better, he was contacted by Jefferson, and told that it was time again to dye his wool.

Lanny just couldn't stand the thought of going through this again.

"I can't" he bleated. "I just can't."

"But you must" Jefferson, said. "If you are to be a member of good standing with the flock, and if you are to be acceptable to the good shepherd, then you must."

Lanny consented. It hurt. It was torture. And in my dream, I again felt what Lanny was feeling. But he could not stand the thought of being and outcast for just one minute, and he believed the discomfort and pain from the dye would be a small price to pay for being accepted.

Once again, sheering time came to the flock.

This time Lanny could not take another round of bleaching. He hurt more this time than he did last time.

As he spoke with the other sheep in his dislocated flock, he learned that it got harder to do rather than easier. "The dye was hard on the skin," they told him, "but in the end, he would see that it was worth it." Lanny wondered if they really believed that.

When approached again about the dye, Lanny refused.

"What?" his friends asked. "What do you mean you're not going to do it again? You're not going to risk being an outcast are you? You're not going to risk the anger of the good shepherd are you?"

But Lanny couldn't bare the thought of more bleach on his skin. It was just too painful.

He took a trip over to see the wise Ram.

The Ram listened to him carefully and then looked at him with great compassion. "I understand what you're going through" he said. "I have seen this before."

"You have?" Lanny asked.

"For some reason nature mixes it up just a bit, I think that it's because she likes variety. But instead of appreciating the added color, her creatures conclude that it's a result of some perversion or some error." Then he looked down at Lanny. "Come" he said. "Follow me."

Lanny followed him, and they walked through the meadow into another pasture.

In this pasture Lanny noticed many sheep, some black and some white, all living and playing together. Nobody seemed to care that they were different. If anything, they enjoyed the differences and made light of them.

When Lanny was introduced, the rest of the flock welcomed him. "Welcome" they all said. "Come join us down at the pond."

Lanny remembered the pond. He had grown to hate the pond because it continued to show him how different he was from his friends and family. But this time the pond made no judgments. He had black wool and nobody else seemed to mind.

Lanny was home, and in my dream I was happy that things finally worked out for him.

Meanwhile the sheep in Lanny's former flock, including his mother and father and brothers and sisters went on with their business never knowing the pain they had caused, and they soon forgot all about Lanny. They cared nothing for him if he would not be like them.

I woke up that morning smiling because I knew that Lanny was going to be okay with his new family. A family that loved him black wool and all.

About the Author

BEN TOUSEY came from a conservative background, and spent most of his life from puberty onward struggling to "overcome" his homosexuality, believing that was the only way to give his life completely over to God and have his dreams fulfilled. Throughout his career Ben has worked as a writer, an actor and a director. He's worked with Grant Goodeve from Eight is Enough and Northern Exposure, Barry McGuire from the Broadway musical Hair and the hit song, "Eve of Destruction." He is the author of several books, including "The Warrior" and "Acting Your Dreams (Using Acting Techniques to Interpret Your Dreams)."

www.ingramcontent.com/pod-product-compliance
Lightning Source LLC
Chambersburg PA
CBHW031232280526
45784CB00004B/1542